THE

Revelation

CONVERSATION

THE

Revelation

CONVERSATION

Inspire Greater
Employee Engagement
by Connecting to Purpose

STEVE CURTIN

Berrett–Koehler Publishers, Inc

Berrett-Koehler Publishers, Inc.
1333 Broadway, Suite 1000
Oakland, CA 94612-1921
Tel: (510) 817-2277
Fax: (510) 817-2278
www.bkconnection.com

ORDERING INFORMATION
Quantity sales. Special discounts are available on quantity purchases by corporations, associations, and others. For details, contact the "Special Sales Department" at the Berrett-Koehler address above.
Individual sales. Berrett-Koehler publications are available through most bookstores. They can also be ordered directly from Berrett-Koehler: Tel: (800) 929-2929; Fax: (802) 864-7626; www.bkconnection.com.
Orders for college textbook / course adoption use. Please contact Berrett-Koehler: Tel: (800) 929-2929; Fax: (802) 864-7626.

Distributed to the U.S. trade and internationally by Penguin Random House Publisher Services.

Berrett-Koehler and the BK logo are registered trademarks of Berrett-Koehler Publishers, Inc.

Printed in the United States of America

Berrett-Koehler books are printed on long-lasting acid-free paper. When it is available, we choose paper that has been manufactured by environmentally responsible processes. These may include using trees grown in sustainable forests, incorporating recycled paper, minimizing chlorine in bleaching, or recycling the energy produced at the paper mill.

Library of Congress Cataloging-in-Publication Data

Name: Curtin, Steve, author.
Title: The revelation conversation : inspire greater employee engagement by
    connecting to purpose / Steve Curtin.
Description: First edition. | Oakland, CA : Berrett-Koehler Publishers, Inc., [2022] |
    Includes bibliographical references and index.
Identifiers: LCCN 2021050953 (print) | LCCN 2021050954 (ebook) |
    ISBN 9781523000678 (paperback) | ISBN 9781523000685 (pdf) |
    ISBN 9781523000692 (epub)
Subjects: LCSH: Employee motivation. | Personnel management. | Work
    Environment—Psychological aspects.
Classification: LCC HF5549.5.M63 .C87 2022 (print) | LCC HF5549.5.M63 (ebook) |
    DDC 658.3/14—dc23/eng/20220112
LC record available at https://lccn.loc.gov/2021050953
LC ebook record available at https://lccn.loc.gov/2021050954

First Edition

27 26 25 24 23 22   10 9 8 7 6 5 4 3 2 1

Book production: Linda Jupiter Productions   Copyedit: Karen Seriguchi
Text design: Lewelin Polanco   Proofread: Mary Kanable
Cover design: Rob Johnson   Index: Lieser Indexing
Author photo: Paul Abdoo Photography

There weren't these two opposites, work and play, one bad and the other good. It was having a vision of the way things ought to be and then making them that way.

—J.W. MARRIOTT SR.

Contents

Introduction

In 2016 I had an experience while working with a sophisticated billion-dollar technology company that, for me, was a *Damascene* moment. (I thought about writing *seminal moment* or *revelation*, but Damascene best describes the sensation of scales falling from my eyes. I imagine it's how Paul the Apostle must have felt when he experienced his conversion on the road to Damascus.) I was invited to speak to a group of senior leaders at the company's annual leadership summit on the topic of connecting to purpose at work. As a part of my preparation for the event, I asked my client how familiar he felt leadership was with the organization's single-sentence mission statement: "We support our clients' efforts to tell stories and make lasting impressions."* He was confident that most of the leaders in attendance would be able to recall it word for word. I suggested a simple activity to verify his hunch.

Prior to my presentation, we distributed three index cards to each of the 222 leaders in attendance. On the first card, they were asked to record the company's one-sentence corporate mission statement. They were instructed to work independently from memory, without the aid of a smartphone or the colleague seated next to

---

* Altered to protect the company's identity.

them. (I'll tell you what we asked them to do with the other two index cards in chapter 2, "The Anatomy of a Job Role.")

Guess what we discovered? Only 4 of the 222 leaders in attendance (less than 2 percent) could accurately recall the company's one-sentence corporate mission statement. Thirty-four participants (15 percent) left their cards blank or answered with a question mark. One senior manager thought it was a trick question and wrote, "As far as I know, we don't have a corporate mission statement right now."

How could that be? My client had suggested that "most" would be able to recall the mission statement verbatim.

This experience reinforced the observation that spurred me to write this book: Although organizations *consistently* develop corporate mission, vision, and purpose statements, leadership is *inconsistently* able to recall them. As a result, leaders are unable to reveal these corporate ideals to employees, connect them to employees' daily job responsibilities, and leverage them to inspire greater employee engagement.

▪ ▪ ▪

Imagine you are leading a group of volunteers who will be going door-to-door to collect donations for hospitalized children. While preparing the volunteers for their assignments, you carefully explain what you want them to do (share the name of the charity and collect donations) and how to do it (canvass neighborhoods, knock on doors, introduce yourself, and explain the cause).

Now, suppose you went a step further. What if you told them something more compelling about *why* their job was so important? What if you shared that the funds would help provide an urgently needed heart transplant for Ethan Nelson, the son of a disabled veteran? What if you showed the volunteers a photo of the father sitting beside his son's hospital bed? Now the volunteers may see their roles as more than just collecting donations. Now they are saving lives. Now they put their heart and soul into the fundraising effort and work even more passionately to collect as much money as possible. And that's because you revealed the totality of their job role. You connected their job to a purpose. You inspired them to go the extra mile to get results.

Studies have long shown that there is a positive correlation between finding meaning in work (the *why*) and engagement with that work.[1] In one study, fundraisers who read stories about the *why* behind their work earned more pledges and raised more money than those who didn't receive information about why their work was important.[2] Like the volunteers going door-to-door to raise funds for Ethan Nelson, most employees want to be engaged in and inspired by their work and workplace. Beyond financial objectives, they are searching for companies, work cultures, and job roles that reflect meaning and purpose and that make a difference. In these organizations, employee engagement, productivity, and customer satisfaction increase, while absenteeism and turnover decrease.[3]

Too often, however, employees are not given sufficient information regarding the relationship between their job responsibilities and the real purpose of their jobs. Even in purpose-driven companies there can be a chasm separating employees from *what* they do and *how* they do it, and *why* they do it. I developed the Revelation Conversation to bridge this gap.

WHAT IS THE REVELATION CONVERSATION?

The Revelation Conversation is a performance management tool designed to support supervisors, managers, and leaders as they, perhaps for the first time, reveal the totality of their employees' job roles, connect their job responsibilities to a purpose, and inspire greater employee engagement. It is a framework for a series of informal one-on-one "revelatory" conversations between leaders and employees to ensure that employees understand the *why* behind their job roles and how that *why* should be reflected in their everyday job tasks. The way I see it, initiating the Revelation Conversation with employees may be the single best use of a supervisor's time at work.

As you may have guessed, the three objectives for the Revelation Conversation are

- to reveal the total job role
- to connect job functions to job purpose
- to inspire greater employee engagement

More often than not, all of the tools to achieve these aims are already at your disposal; they're just not being utilized effectively—or at all. For instance, even though every job role has multiple dimensions, most employees are only aware of one. And the job role's purpose always exists, whether or not it has been articulated by leadership and linked to workers' daily job responsibilities. Most people prefer to be *on board* and inspired at work rather than *just bored* and going through the motions. Each of these levers is just awaiting discovery and activation.

WHY I WROTE THIS BOOK

After a twenty-year career at Marriott International, I launched a consulting firm with a purpose to raise customer service quality from ordinary to extraordinary. That was back in 2007. In 2013 my book *Delight Your Customers* was published.[4] The book introduced three truths of exceptional customer service and seven simple ways to improve customer service quality.

The inspiration to write the book came from this observation: Although employees *consistently* execute the mandatory "job functions" for which they are paid, they *inconsistently* demonstrate the voluntary "job essence" for which there is little or no additional cost to their employer. I use the term *job functions* to describe the duties and tasks associated with a job role, and the term *job essence* to describe the actions and behaviors that support and reflect employees' job purpose, their single highest priority at work.

Simon Sinek got it right when he wrote his best-selling book *Start with Why*.⁵ It was influential in challenging me to dig deeper into the root causes of employee indifference and transactional, process-focused customer service. As a result, in the years since *Delight Your Customers* was published, the focus of my consulting work has shifted from *what* companies should do to improve customer service quality and *how* they should do it, to strengthening employees' motivation to do it. *Why* do employees do what they do the way they do it? That's how the Revelation Conversation was born.

Revealing the *why*, the true purpose of one's job role, is critical to inspiring greater employee engagement and performance. Throughout the book I am careful to differentiate between life purpose and job purpose—they are not the same thing, and they don't need to be in order to have engaged, high-performing employees. I'll explain why in chapter 1, "Purpose at Work: The Two Journeys." I have consulted with a diverse set of clients, many of whom you will meet in these pages, from a multibillion-dollar cruise line, retailers, hospitals, and hotel companies, to tourism boards, government entities, and public library networks. These organizations serve customers, guests, clients, members, users, subscribers, partners, patients, patrons, donors, visitors, residents, and citizens.* Through their examples, I will show how you can initiate Revelation Conversations that will enlighten your employees, make job purpose actionable, and spur team enthusiasm, commitment, and performance.

HOW TO USE THIS BOOK

The book is organized into three parts, each focused on one of the three levers of the Revelation Conversation. It is best to read the book sequentially rather than skip around, as each part builds on the

---

* In this book, I will predominantly refer to the recipients of your service as "customers," although you may call them something else. I will also use the term *customer service*, acknowledging that you may prefer *guest service*, *client service*, or other variation.

preceding part(s) until its conclusion. For instance, it will not be possible to initiate the Revelation Conversation in part II without first realizing the totality of a job role from part I.

Part I: Revealing the Total Job Role

In part I, I explain the key differences between life purpose and job purpose—this book is about the latter—and dissect a job role to uncover a dimension of every job role that is often invisible to employees and their supervisors.

While most people are aware of what their job functions are, the true purpose of their job remains elusive. Employees regularly view the totality of their job role in terms of possessing job knowledge and demonstrating job skills. They are often oblivious to the greater *why* behind *what* they do, and *how* they do it. Employees who work in these environments routinely process customers, each one like the one before, until the end of another boring and monotonous shift. They leave each day unenthusiastic, uninspired, and unengaged.

Now, there will always be a percentage of engaged employees who go above and beyond in the service of their customers, regardless of whether their job purpose has been articulated, shared, and modeled by their immediate supervisors. Encounters with these employees are what I call "happy accidents." This is when you just *happen* to get a knowledgeable phone rep, an effervescent waitress, or a detail-oriented house painter. In other words, the customer's experience hinges on the employee they *happen* to encounter.

But relying on happy accidents is not a formula for success. This book aims to transform inconsistent happy accidents that are *reliant on the employee involved*, into consistently superior customer experiences *regardless of the employee involved*. The first step in this process is to reveal the totality of employees' job roles, including job purpose.

Part II: Connecting Job Functions to Job Purpose

In part II, I walk through the process of initiating the Revelation Conversation, an informal discussion between a supervisor and an employee about how their daily job responsibilities connect to the purpose of the job role. I will explore how answering the following Four Questions lays the foundation for that first conversation.

1. What is my purpose at work?
2. What values guide my actions and behaviors at work?
3. What purposeful actions and behaviors do I exhibit at work?
4. What is my team's aspirational goal?

Then, I will dive deeper into how to manifest job purpose through deliberate actions and discretionary behaviors that can be operationalized by incorporating them into systems, processes, and daily responsibilities. The goal is to execute reliably, over time, by design rather than inconsistently, here and there, by chance.

Part III: Inspiring Greater Employee Engagement

Once employees are made aware of the totality of their job roles, can state their purpose at work, and are able to connect their daily actions and behaviors to that purpose, it is the supervisor's role to keep that connection alive in ways that inspire greater employee engagement and team performance. In part III, I offer examples of how specific purposeful actions and behaviors, serving as leading indicators, can influence individual and team performance, achieve key performance indicator (KPI) targets, and initiate progress toward the team's aspirational goal. It is crucial that employees can see how their efforts correlate to KPIs that are tracked and measured by the organization—this is how you create interest, momentum, and excitement in the pursuit of purpose at work.

Beyond the numbers and tracking, purpose-driven leaders also behave in ways that inspire those around them, such as displaying enthusiasm and optimism while arousing team spirit. As I will explain in chapter 7, "Creating Team Alignment," collaborating with your team to create a credible, actionable rallying cry can align efforts and inspire team members to transcend the daily routine and keep their focus on the aspirational goal.

Reflection Questions and Exercises

At the end of each chapter, I include tested consulting questions and activities to reveal the total job role, link employee actions and behaviors to corporate ideals, and inspire greater employee engagement. I encourage you to pause at these points before moving on to the next chapter. Take some time to answer these questions for yourself, your team, and your organization. Who knows? They may contribute to your own Damascene moment. And when you reach chapter 4, "Initiating the Revelation Conversation," these answers will prepare you to confidently hold Revelation Conversations with your staff.

WHY YOU SHOULD READ THIS BOOK

The Revelation Conversation is for leaders at all levels of an organization who want to be seen as credible, purpose-driven leaders in the eyes of those whom they lead. Why? Because uninformed leaders who are disconnected from their purpose at work do not inspire employee confidence or engagement.

I wrote this book to help you bridge the knowledge gap between what your organization stands for and how that conviction informs the daily behavior and decision-making of employees. It will help you to develop enlightened and engaged employees who understand what their job purpose is and how they can act on it for improved performance. And its guidance has the potential, when applied, to create team alignment and inspire the collective pursuit of a common aspirational goal.

Let's see what's behind the curtain.

PART I

Revealing the Total Job Role

1 | Purpose at Work: The Two Journeys

N orman Lear is a renowned American television writer and producer behind many of the 1970s' most popular sitcoms, including *All in the Family*, *Sanford and Son*, and *The Jeffersons*. He is also known for his profound comments about how the desire to lead a more purposeful life, to search for ultimate meanings, is a central theme of the human experience.

"I think that we're on two journeys," observed Mr. Lear. "We are on a horizontal journey, and we are on a vertical journey. A horizontal journey is, I'm studying this, I'm studying that, I'm learning more about all of these things as life goes on. The vertical journey is into oneself and into the meaning of oneself and one's being. That is the longer, I find, and perhaps more rewarding in a spiritual sense, [the] more rewarding journey."[1]

That imagery resonates with me. I think he's right that there are two journeys: a journey of self-improvement and a journey of self-discovery. The latter journey is the one that (ideally) leads you to your existential purpose in life.

It is healthy to be introspective and to think deeply about the purpose of your life. People who self-reflect, determine where their passions lie, and crystalize a purpose for their life tend to concentrate their effort and energy on what matters most. A clear purpose provides a foundation on which to base decisions, allocate your time, and use your resources. And there are documented health benefits for those who cite having a clear purpose about what makes their lives meaningful, such as fewer strokes and heart attacks, better sleep, and a lower risk of dementia.[2] People with a sense of purpose, a sense of control, and a feeling that what they do is worthwhile, also tend to live longer.[3]

That said, most people are unaware of their purpose in life. Only around 25 percent of Americans cite having a clear sense of purpose about what makes their lives meaningful.[4] They haven't done the work or, more accurately, they are unaware of the work to be done to discover their purpose. And those who are attuned to their life's purpose may spend a lifetime coaxing it out of the universe.

Although a good chunk of us may never discover our existential purpose in life, that's not true for organizations. They have a responsibility to identify and articulate their purpose from their beginnings, usually in the form of mission, vision, and purpose statements. Organizations must be intentional about their purpose, communicate it to employees at all levels of the organization, and imbue it in every process, including job design, employee selection, onboarding, and performance management.

In contrast to much that has been written on the topic, I disagree that organizations should endeavor to align their employees' life purpose with their purpose at work. It's not that it's impossible. But it is exceedingly difficult, costly, and time-consuming, not to mention presumptuous, as I'll explain. Especially in industries that experience high turnover and labor shortages, attempting to align employees' life purpose with the purpose of their job role is an exercise in futility.

There are, as always, exceptions. One American health care company uses an app for its people to make connections between their personal values and life purpose and the values and purpose of the organization. An Asian insurance company devotes time in its leadership programs to reflect on the link between employees' individual life purpose and that of the corporation. And in an effort to reexamine its purpose, a Scandinavian bank listened to more than seven thousand people in and around its organization over a period of six months in workshops, via online surveys, and in more than 1,500 coffee corner discussions.[5] If your organization has the time and expertise to execute similar initiatives and feels it is the best use of your limited resources, then don't let me discourage you. In this book, however, my focus will be on purpose at work, not life purpose. Specifically, I will challenge you to articulate for your employees a credible job purpose and to make it an actionable part of their job roles.

Part I, "Revealing the Total Job Role," consists of chapters 1 and 2. The objective of chapter 1 is for the reader to be able to distinguish between people's existential life purpose and their purpose at work. These are often melded to form a single convoluted and inaccurate view of one's purpose at work. The objective of chapter 2, "The Anatomy of a Job Role," is for the reader to be able to reveal the totality of an employee's job role, which includes two dimensions and three parts. Here, I will illustrate how job purpose completes the third, often overlooked, element of every job role.

JOB PURPOSE VERSUS LIFE PURPOSE

Job purpose is a job role's reason for being. It unifies team members by clarifying their single highest priority at work and pointing them toward an aspirational goal. For example, the job purpose of servers at a high-end restaurant might be to surprise and delight every customer. Think about your own experience as a diner. Can you recall an evening when an interesting chef's taste was brought to your table, or an engaged sommelier made connections between your global travels and the region from which the wine you chose originated? Or when you had a tableside chat with a charming restaurant manager, received a complimentary dessert and, perhaps, even a card signed by the staff on your birthday? Or when your conscientious server directed you to the gluten-free options or recommended that the kitchen hold the beurre blanc sauce to accommodate your intolerance for dairy?

There is a tendency to be overly literal in ascribing a job role's purpose by suggesting, for example, that a housekeeper's job purpose must be linked to cleanliness, a flight attendant's job purpose must pertain to safety, and an accountant's job purpose must relate to accuracy. A job role's purpose is not the technical or literal reason a job role exists in the same way that one's life purpose is not merely to continue breathing. A job purpose is a role's *aspirational* reason for being. It's the job role's North Star.

Although there is merit to examining both job and life purpose, anticipating a match is not realistic. It is presumptuous, even arrogant, to expect that employees' life purpose will align with their purpose at work and that the degree to which there's a match, indicates a good fit. To expect alignment ignores the fact that one's life purpose is intensely personal and unknowable to many employers. One's life purpose is unique, even singular. As Viktor Frankl wrote in *Man's Search for Meaning*: "Life ultimately means taking the responsibility to find the right answer to its problems and to fulfill the tasks which it constantly sets for each individual. These tasks, and therefore the meaning of life, differ from [person to person] and from moment to moment."[6] He concludes that a person's search for meaning "is unique and specific in that it must and can be fulfilled by [him or her] alone."[7]

Now let's say someone has done the work and that after hours of contemplation and weeks of rewrites, arrives at the following statement of purpose for their life: "My life's purpose is to live my truth, uninhibited by fear, and to live authentically."

I doubt that this life purpose, which is not an outlier, is aligned with the purposes of most organizations. This reality should not disqualify this person from having a rewarding career at a company whose purpose does not include references to truth, fearlessness, or authenticity.

You may be thinking, "But what about a calling? Doesn't that imply alignment between one's life and job purpose?" It might be useful at this juncture to clarify some terms that often get blurred in these discussions:

- A *hobby or avocation (elective)* you do for enjoyment. It's fun.
- A *job (necessity)*, whether or not it's enjoyable and fulfilling, you do in order to earn money to pay for things.
- A *career (status)* is an occupation that is undertaken for a significant period of your life. It's rewarding to the extent that it's enjoyable, fulfilling, and affirming.
- A *vocation (meaning)* is a sacred calling and is not dependent on anyone else. Unlike a job, it cannot be taken away from you. A symphony might lose its funding, an art studio might close, and a publication may cease printing. Nevertheless, as Abraham Maslow wrote, "A musician must make music, an artist must paint, a poet must write, if he is to be ultimately happy."[8]

And now, to answer the question above: Yes, I do believe a person's job purpose and calling, or vocation, *can* be one and the same. However, they don't *have* to be for an employee to be engaged and fulfilled at work. And, most importantly, companies shouldn't expect it or even strive for it. As Derek Thompson observed in *The Atlantic*, "It's hard to self-actualize on the job if you're a cashier—one of the most common occupations in the US—and even the best white-collar roles have long periods of stasis, boredom, or busywork."[9] The overwhelming majority of employees come to work to trade their time for compensation. In other words, they have a job—not a calling. And that's okay. Their work can still be purposeful.

People have limitless imagination with which to imbue their work with meaning and purpose. You might recall the oft-told story about the mason who did not see his job as laying bricks, but rather as building a cathedral. Or the tale of the janitor at NASA who told President Kennedy that he did not see his job as mopping floors, but rather as helping to send a man to the moon. These stories show that a fulfilling job purpose is not reserved for the arts or sacred callings. It is also not limited to volunteer or cause organizations, nonprofits, or B Corporations that aspire to balance profit and purpose. No matter the job role, articulating its purpose can lead to greater engagement within the role and organization.

To return to Mr. Lear's two journeys, think of your own life in terms of a horizontal journey of self-improvement and a vertical journey of self-discovery. These journeys are concurrent. You are on both journeys even while you're at work or reading a book like this one that is intended for self-development. What distinguishes these journeys is that only one of them is readily available to your employer. For instance, when you are in nature contemplating your existential purpose in life, you are primarily on a vertical journey "into the meaning of oneself and one's being." Here you may be alone, and your reflections and discoveries are deeply personal. When you are at work, however, you are primarily on a horizontal journey "studying this, studying that, and learning more about all of these things." Your coworkers are also on their own journeys. Although their vertical journey of self-discovery is private and inaccessible (unless they choose to share it), their horizontal journey of self-improvement is awaiting your input and guidance.

It's my ambition, with this book, to focus on the horizontal journey, the very real opportunities that managers and leaders have to influence their employees' journey of self-development at work, improve business outcomes, and inspire greater employee engagement.

EMPLOYEE ENGAGEMENT AND JOB PURPOSE

It's no secret that most employees are disengaged at work. The same troubling statistics are compiled and released monthly by Gallup and other workplace analytics companies. As of this writing, the latest Gallup survey found that only 36 percent of employees are engaged at work.[10] And the situation is even more bleak internationally, with global employee engagement decreasing by 2 percentage points from 2019 to 2020 to only 20 percent. Employee engagement in Latin America and the Caribbean averaged 24 percent, Southeast Asia averaged 23 percent, Eastern Europe 21 percent, Australia and New Zealand 20 percent, and Middle East and North Africa 16 percent.[11] The UK and Western Europe have the lowest employee engagement levels globally at just 11 percent.[12]

Gallup's analysis of US employee engagement reveals that gains have been made over the past two decades as corporations invested in engagement surveys, employee wellness programs, and other levers designed to increase employee engagement and retention. Even so, are we really content with only a third of American workers being highly involved in, enthusiastic about, and committed to their work and workplace while the other two-thirds are either not engaged or, worse, actively disengaged. Employees who are not engaged are psychologically unattached to their work and company. These employees put time, but not energy or passion, into their work. They typically show up to work and contribute the minimum effort required. They are also on the lookout for better employment opportunities and will quickly leave their company for a slightly better offer.

Actively disengaged employees make up, on average, three out of every twenty employees. These employees aren't just unhappy at work; they are resentful that their needs aren't being met and are acting out their unhappiness while enduring miserable work experiences and spreading their unhappiness to their colleagues.[13]

Organizations pay a hefty price for disengaged employees in increased turnover, absenteeism, and shrinkage (loss, theft, breakage) and in decreased productivity, profitability, and customer loyalty. Gallup estimates that low employee engagement costs the global economy $8.1 trillion yearly with the lost productivity of a single unengaged or actively disengaged employee equal to 18 percent of their annual salary. So, for a company with ten thousand employees with an average salary of $50,000 each, disengagement costs $60.3 million a year. Furthermore, replacing a single worker requires one-half to two times the employee's annual salary. In other words, it costs $9,000 a year to keep each disengaged worker and between $25,000 and $100,000 to replace them.[14]

Although it is true that the single greatest contributing factor to employee engagement is an employee's immediate supervisor, there are plenty of other factors, many of which are beyond a manager's control. One of the keys to effectiveness is to focus on that which you can control. If you are frustrated by the traffic you encounter on the way into work, blowing your horn during rush hour won't help. You cannot control traffic. Your progress will be limited to that of the car in front of yours. There are, however, choices that are within your control to mitigate the effects of traffic. You can access an app that will tell you exactly how long it will take to arrive at your destination. This will help you to reset expectations. The same app can provide you with alternative routes that may reduce the amount of traffic you encounter, saving you time. You can also adjust your departure time to avoid traffic. Or you can choose to listen to an audiobook or music that gives you a sense of calm and reduces the stress associated with traffic.

When you think about purpose in the workplace, think about what you have control over as a leader or manager. Hint: It's not an employee's life purpose. In the context of Norman Lear's two journeys, you can directly impact employees' horizontal journey of self-improvement, while their vertical journey of self-discovery, much like your own, is reliant on their *individual* exploration of unique talents, interests, and experiences.

So, tapping into employees' life purpose is outside the purview of this book, but there are many purpose-driven employee engagement strategies that we will explore, including

- revealing the total job role
- articulating and championing job purpose
- connecting job functions to job purpose
- making time for regular, informal one-on-one conversations with employees regarding job purpose
- identifying and tracking purposeful actions and behaviors that positively influence company KPIs
- developing a workgroup-specific aspirational goal and rallying cry

Let's talk a little more about those one-on-ones. Several years ago, I discovered a tool—a framework for a series of ongoing one-on-one conversations—that has the potential to reveal the totality of an employee's job role (including job purpose), to connect their job responsibilities to that purpose, and in doing so, to inspire greater employee engagement. I call it the Revelation Conversation. Next, in preparation for having these conversations, we'll explore the two dimensions and three parts of every job role and the potential that is unleashed when you can give employees the full picture of what their job entails.

Exercise

Below is a set of questions that will help you assess your awareness of your employer's ideals and clarify your current view of a job role. Recording your responses to these questions now will be useful

when, at the end of the next chapter, you revisit them and compare
your responses.

1. Recall from memory, without the aid of a smartphone
   or other resource, your organization's mission, vision,
   or purpose statement:

   _____

   _____

   _____

2. Describe, from your perspective, your job role
   (i.e., what your job entails):

   - _____
   - _____
   - _____
   - _____
   - _____
   - _____
   - _____

3. If you manage or supervise others, what do you see as
   your employees' single highest priority at work? If you
   are an individual contributor, with no direct reports,
   what do you see as your own single highest priority at
   work?

   _____

   _____

   _____

2 | The Anatomy of a Job Role

D avid Dunning, a Cornell professor of social psychology, was thumbing through the 1996 *World Almanac* when he came across an account of two unusual bank robberies that occurred the previous year in Pittsburgh, Pennsylvania. What made them peculiar was that, judging from the surveillance video, the suspect in the robberies made no attempt to disguise himself. When he was arrested, McArthur Wheeler was incredulous. "But I wore the juice," he said. Having coated his face with lemon juice, he assumed his identity would be invisible to security cameras as long as he did not encounter a heat source.[1]

After reading the story, Professor Dunning wondered whether it was possible to measure people's *self-assessed* competence against their *actual* competence. Within weeks, he and a graduate student, Justin Kruger, had organized a research study that resulted in the 1999 paper "Unskilled and Unaware of It."[2]

The paper reveals that when we don't know a particular fact or lack the skill to do something well, we don't know enough to accurately assess our ability. This phenomenon results in an illusion of expertise that assured at least one bank robber that lemon juice would conceal his identity and convinces the rest of us that we're better than average drivers, parents, or investors. One nationwide survey found that 21 percent of Americans believe that it's "very likely" or "fairly likely" that they'll become millionaires within the next ten years.[3] Given that, as of 2020, only 9 percent of Americans were millionaires, this overly optimistic assessment of one's financial acumen seems to validate the team's findings.[4]

As Professor Dunning explains, "Even if you are just the most honest, impartial person that you could be, you would still have a problem—namely, when your knowledge or expertise is imperfect, you really don't know it. Left to our own devices, you just don't know it. We're not very good at knowing what we don't know."[5] This illusion of confidence became known as the Dunning-Kruger effect.

This may explain why my client from the introduction, convinced that "most" of the senior managers could recall the company's one-sentence mission statement, was unaware of the reality of the situation (less than 2 percent could).

I hope that I am not sounding overly critical of Mr. Wheeler and my client. The truth is that even though I should have known better, having researched the Dunning-Kruger effect for this book, I still overestimated my ability to meet a July 1 deadline to deliver the draft manuscript. After receiving an extension from my editor to July 5, I contacted him early that morning to negotiate a new deadline of September 17. My wife was dismayed. She said, "You missed your original deadline by seventy-eight days? How is that even possible?" And she had a good point. I goofed. I had overestimated my abilities. I had succumbed to the cognitive bias of illusory superiority that I was cautioning others against. Shame.

Here's another personal example. I recall the first PowerPoint presentation I created and would like to use this opportunity to formally apologize to those unsuspecting audience members at the New York Marriott Marquis in 1997. The presentation was based on the book *Inside the Magic Kingdom* by Tom Connellan.[6] Toward the end of the book, the author recapped the seven keys to Disney's success and included discussion questions. I typed each one of these out on its own slide, some containing more than seventy words. And I didn't stop there. I maximized PowerPoint's brilliance by using fade-ins, fade-outs, and cut-across slide transitions. And I thought it was a good idea to animate each letter in the header introducing the next key to success so that the sentence appeared one letter at a time.

That was the decade during which the training world migrated from acetates and overhead projectors to presentation software and LCD projectors. Had you asked me at the time for a self-critique, I would have said my presentation was state of the art and that learner retention likely increased due to the interest stimulated by the dazzling presentation effects. Fast-forward twenty-four years and I can easily spot my foibles, at least as they pertain to PowerPoint. But if you were to interview colleagues, clients, audience members, blog readers, and others who have been on the receiving end of my art lately, there is no doubt you would uncover instances where I have overestimated my own abilities relative to others'.

According to Professor Dunning, who now teaches at the University of Michigan, the Dunning-Kruger effect explains why so many people underperform at their job. Like Mr. Wheeler, my client, and me, they may not know that they could be doing better or what really great performance looks like.[7] In other words, most people don't know what they don't know about their job role. And so, we make assumptions about what we believe to be true and blindly act on those hunches without regard to the facts.

BEING COMPETENT IS NOT ENOUGH

In the absence of more information, employees mistake a partial view of their job role as being complete. And it is this limited perspective that informs their assessment of their job performance—their competency. Aspiring to manage competent employees is fine if your objective is for them to process customers, treating each one like the previous one, until the end of another routine and predictable shift. But if your aim is to inspire them in the collective pursuit of a common aspirational goal, then having competent employees is not nearly enough.

Whenever I ask five frontline service providers in the same job role, individually, to describe for me—from their perspective—their job role and what it entails, their responses are dominated by job functions. For example, contact center workers will often describe their job role as answering incoming calls, responding to emails, handling customer inquiries, researching required information, resolving complaints, processing orders, escalating priority issues, routing calls, completing call logs, and producing call reports. Often, there is no mention of job purpose—or the actions and behaviors that reflect that purpose.

When I ask the same five employees to share the purpose of their job role, their single highest priority at work, confusion ensues. I get dumbfounded looks followed by, "What do you mean?" or "Could you repeat the question?"

Without elaborating, I simply restate the question: "What is your job purpose, your single highest priority at work?"

After an awkward pause and some stammering, workers will attempt to select the "correct" answer. In doing so, they will reluctantly offer responses in the form of questions like, "Customer service?," "Quality?," "Productivity?," "Sales?," or "Safety?" Or they will choose a particular key performance indicator (KPI) that has been receiving a lot of attention lately. At a contact center, this might be "first call resolution" or "average handle time."

Although their responses are noble, the fact that they are all different exposes the problem. Remember, the question was not, "What is *one of your priorities* at work?" The question was, "What is your purpose at work, your *single highest priority*?"

What these subtle experiments have shown me is that most employees in the same job role are on the same page as to *what* they're supposed to do and *how* they're supposed to do it, but there is a lack of awareness about *why* they do what they do, the way they do it—their job purpose. As a result, many competent employees lack purpose at work and unwittingly cap their potential.

My work has shown me that when employees are made aware of the totality of their job role, their connection to their work expands. When employees are connected to something more than executing transactions and processing customers, they are liberated to bring their whole selves to work, to fully engage.

WHAT'S IN A JOB ROLE?

Most business leaders would agree that work is more fulfilling when employees know that what they do matters and are aware of how their daily contributions connect to purpose. Yet a gap exists between leadership's stated and actual priorities. In reality, most leaders aren't even talking with employees about job purpose.

When newly hired workers transition into a company, it is the responsibility of their immediate supervisor to reveal the totality of their particular job role. Of course, for the supervisor to do that, they must also be aware of the totality of their own job role. Unfortunately, in most cases supervisors—and the management levels above them—have the same incomplete view of their job role.

So, what's in a job role? Let's start with the easy, familiar part: job functions.

Job functions, as noted in the introduction, pertain to the duties and tasks associated with a job role. This dimension of a job role consists of *job knowledge*, such as hours of operation, product specifications, pricing, and availability, and *job skills*. These skills can be technical, such as keyboarding, operating point of sale software, or programming, or soft skills such as communications, customer service, or time management. Job functions inform employees about *what* to do and *how* to do it. They are mandatory, often transactional, process focused, and generally expected by customers. The manager's real world of work tends to be defined by the instruments of job function, including job descriptions, checklists, standards, policies, procedures, protocols, procurement forms, daily operations reports, quotas, budgets, performance appraisals, and productivity reports.

The other, more elusive dimension of a job role is job essence. Job essence, as indicated in the introduction, describes the actions and behaviors that support and reflect employees' job purpose.

Job purpose, as we've been discussing, is the single highest priority of the job role. It is displayed in the choreographed actions and voluntary, relational, people-focused behaviors of employees. These are the oftentimes unexpected little "extras" that elevate an experience from ordinary to extraordinary, a customer from satisfied to delighted, and an employee from indifferent to engaged. Figure 1 illustrates the elements of a job role.

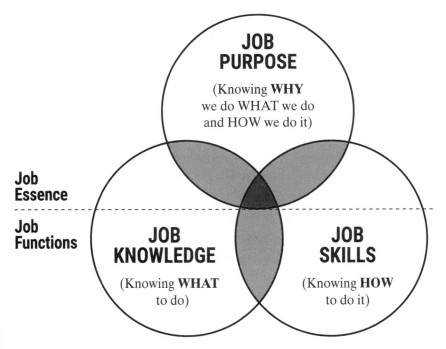

Figure 1: The Anatomy of a Job Role

From this description, one might think that executing job functions should be subordinated to performing actions and behaviors that reflect job purpose. After all, in contrast to job functions, job purpose is composed of largely "voluntary, relational, people-focused" behaviors that can "elevate an experience from ordinary to extraordinary." Naturally, job essence should be the priority, right? There is a (false) assumption that customer-centric organizations like Disney and Nordstrom myopically focus on delighting the customer and deemphasize routine and predictable job functions. But it's not zero-sum, executing job functions or reflecting job purpose. It's both.

This book doesn't spend much time on job functions, and that's by design. Management is already versed in policies and procedures, performance standards, utilization metrics, and financial reports that govern the world of job functions. And employees are generally competent. I'm not here to teach managers and employees how to be more efficient or how to increase their competency. That's the role of the training professionals within their organizations who are consistently producing a legion of employees equipped to reliably execute their job responsibilities and satisfy customers. My intent is to help leaders and employees understand that attention to both job functions *and* job essence is vital to raising performance and engagement levels at work.

Taking it one important step further, I believe the real magic happens when you can incorporate job essence *into* job functions. Consider how job purpose can be reflected, informally, in job functions—apart from a documented process that is tracked and measured by management. The success of a supermarket, for example, hinges on the store's cleanliness and the quality or freshness of perishables like produce, meats, baked goods, and dairy items. If a supermarket employee's job purpose is to "Make everything fresh," then a routine task such as stocking yogurt provides an opportunity to reflect job purpose by rotating existing inventory to reduce the odds that a customer will encounter a product that is out of date.

After all, expired product is inconsistent with freshness. We'll discuss this in detail in chapter 5, "Aligning Actions and Behaviors with Purpose." For now, here's another example to illustrate the point.

The University of Disneyland was founded in 1955 by Van Arsdale France, who was asked to craft a purpose statement for Disneyland. For his presentation to Walt and Roy Disney, Mr. France said, "My goal, as I saw it, was to get everyone we hired to share in an intangible dream, and not just working for a paycheck."[8]

With the Disney brothers and other top executives waiting expectantly, Mr. France told them, "The purpose of Disneyland is to create happiness for others.* . . . [Y]ou may park cars, clean up the place, sweep the place, work graveyard and everything else, but whatever you do is contributing to creating happiness for others."[9]

Bruce Jones, former senior cast development and quality assurance director at the Disney Institute, believes that "Van's particular genius was to create a single, unifying principle that connects every cast member [Disney's term for its employees] with our guests' emotional aspirations. He explained that the common purpose is the raison d'être—the reason for being—and it drives the extraordinary effort, creativity, teamwork, and guest focus for which Disney is known."[10]

Its purpose establishes a parkwide standard of vigilance and awareness so that, when a cast member spots a park guest whose popcorn has spilled on the ground, she knows that replacing that popcorn will "create happiness" more than prioritizing the spill and rushing to get a broom and dustpan. After the guest's popcorn has been replaced and the "magic" restored, there will be plenty of time to tend to that spill.

Disneyland has earned a reputation for going to extraordinary lengths in pursuit of its organizational purpose. One example of how

---

* Disney's purpose has evolved since 1955, though has remained true to its founding purpose. Its current purpose statement reads: "We create happiness by providing the finest in entertainment for people of all ages, everywhere."

it reflects this purpose, its single highest priority — to create happiness for others — during the daily execution of job functions is demonstrated in the way workers are trained to pay fantastic attention to detail. You can see this in its maintenance program for the seventeen hitching posts that line Main Street, U.S.A. at Disneyland. "The high wear points on these horse-head hitching posts are stripped down and repainted every night. . . . Not only [that], the starting time is based on the temperature and humidity, so the paint will be dry by the time the park opens the next morning."[11]

It's easy to criticize this level of detail as obsessive and a waste of resources. However, a company that will pay that much attention to a hitching post will pay close attention to anything that comes in contact with its guests, because attention to detail is part of its culture. Every time a member of the maintenance team inspects and touches up a hitching post, it sends a clear message to other cast members that Disneyland's purpose and values are not platitudes that are disconnected from one's daily job role. It reinforces the legitimacy of those values and the relationship between a job function (park maintenance) and purposeful actions (hypervigilant maintenance schedule) and behaviors (pay fantastic attention to detail) in support of its purpose (to create happiness for others).

WHY PURPOSE AT WORK IS SO ELUSIVE

In the introduction, I referred to a learning activity I conducted with 222 senior leaders from a sophisticated billion-dollar technology company. I provided instructions for attendees to jot down on an index card the company's single-sentence corporate mission statement. As you might recall, less than 2 percent of the leaders in attendance could do so.

On a second index card, I asked them to describe, from their perspective, their job role — what their jobs entailed — in five to seven bullet points. The vast majority of responses, 86 percent, pertained to job functions, the duties and tasks associated with one's job role. These functions involved managing, staffing, problem solving, forecasting, strategizing, traveling, and so on. Only 14 percent related to job essence, actions and behaviors that reflect an employee's job purpose, their single highest priority at work. These included relationship building, delighting customers, and going the extra mile.

On a third index card, I asked them to record their employees' single highest priority at work. Seventy percent of their responses pertained to job functions and only 30 percent were linked to job essence, purposeful actions and behaviors. It was telling that, although the leaders presided over similar operations across the country, they identified more than a dozen *single* highest priorities.

Later, during my presentation, I revisited this question, suggesting these senior leaders pose it to their employees: "What is your single highest priority at work?"

Then I asked the group, "What would you want them to say?"

The group shared aspirational responses that they would hope to hear from employees, such as safety, customer service, quality, productivity, sales, profits, cost containment, and teamwork.

Then I asked the group, "How would they know to say it?"

This is a sobering question because it exposes factors that are often overlooked or insufficiently practiced in day-to-day business. These encompass employee treatment, customer treatment, leadership modeling, communication, feedback, recognition, reinforcement of standards, and providing tangible evidence that the corporate mission, vision, or purpose is more than just a banner that hangs in the employee cafeteria. Collectively, these factors will influence whether or not corporate ideals are viewed by employees as credible, relevant, and enduring.

Employees are pretty observant; they don't miss much. The actions and behaviors they see modeled and those ideals their immediate supervisor appears to value will inform their own behavior and decisions at work. If they see a management team that prioritizes tasks, efficiencies, and productivity (job functions), then that's what they will focus on—often at the expense of purposeful actions and behaviors (job essence).

If an organization does not have a definable purpose that can be articulated by its management team, it cannot measure progress toward it. In every organization, whether people realize it or not, there is a systemic relationship between purpose (*why* we do something), the work itself (*what* we do), and the methods used (*how* we do it). In the absence of a clearly defined and understood purpose at work, other priorities (usually job functions) fill the void, edging out any broader purpose—often with the imperative to "hit the numbers." In these instances, employees go to work with the objective to reliably execute job assignments rather than with a mission to achieve a higher purpose. They're given a task to work on rather than a purpose to work toward.

Work is more fulfilling when employees know that what they do makes a difference, that their jobs have purpose and meaning. This is not a romantic notion. The problem is that in most organizations purpose and meaning are elusive and difficult to define, measure, and pursue. Managers that discount the relevance of meaning in the workplace may lack it themselves, as my example above shows. Most managers are not even aware of their own job purpose, much less how it translates into job essence (purposeful actions and behaviors). And if managers are disconnected from purpose at work, then how can their subordinates reasonably be expected to consistently reflect job purpose in their own actions and behaviors? The inability of leadership to articulate job purpose and model it themselves results in employees being detached from purpose as well.

Here are three reasons why managers are disconnected from job purpose:

Job functions are visible and concrete. Managers can see them, touch them, and measure them daily. They are a real, relevant, and credible part of managers' world of work, whereas job purpose is nebulous, abstract, difficult to see clearly, and tough to articulate. And it comes up only now and then (e.g., annual all-employee meeting, customer service week, or new-hire orientation). Ongoing conversation about job purpose are rare. We're all too busy talking about job functions and concerning ourselves with quotas, productivity, and other metrics. There's no doubt about the importance of job functions. Additionally, managers tend to focus almost exclusively on job functions because they're what their bosses tend to focus on.

Job purpose is poorly defined—if at all. It is seldom articulated in words, modeled by leadership, or intentionally connected to employees' daily job responsibilities. At most, it may be relegated to the employee handbook, a laminated wallet card, an annual report, the company website, or a plaque in the executive corridor.

There are no tools, processes, or mechanisms by which managers encounter or are prompted to interact with job purpose—until the Revelation Conversation. So, any early progress or enthusiasm following an event that showcases job purpose quickly loses momentum as job functions reassume center stage.

For insight into the motivation of managers at most companies, listen to the questions asked of budding entrepreneurs during any episode of *Shark Tank*, where contestants get to pitch their product or business idea to a panel of seasoned investors. The overwhelming percentage of questions are linked to job functions:

- What does it cost to make?
- What do you sell it for?
- What have you sold?
- What is your profit margin?
- Do you have any data on customer acquisition costs?
- How much money have you invested in the company?
- What is the active user base?
- How many subscriptions do you have?
- What is the subscription cost?
- What are net sales after returns?
- What does your capitalization table look like?
- How much cash do you have in the bank?

- How much inventory do you have?
- What's your monthly burn?
- Do you have a patent?
- Where are you selling your product now?
- Where are you manufacturing your product?

It's not that the sharks (investors) don't care about job purpose or corporate ideals. They need to be efficient. Each forty-three-minute episode includes four pitches that are scrutinized by six celebrity investors before offers are extended (or withheld). With little more than ten edited minutes per pitch, there's hardly time for more than the fundamental questions that determine whether or not a deal gets done. Contestants have also been conditioned to focus on job functions by business school professors, bankers, investors, and by watching *Shark Tank* themselves.

Now, let's reflect on your own focus at work. What questions do you tend to ask? What priorities do you emphasize? What expectations do you convey? Consider your last meeting agenda. What percentage of it pertained to job functions versus job purpose?

I once worked for the general manager of a customer-centric hotel who would end a meeting if five minutes elapsed without anyone mentioning the customer. And his focus was reflected in the hotel's customer service and employee engagement levels.

Let's say you are staying at this hotel and call the front desk to request more towels. The front desk agent answers your call, notes the request, and then, after your call ends, contacts housekeeping to fulfill the request. So far, the front desk agent has demonstrated competency in executing her job functions. She has answered the phone, noted the request orally (perhaps even jotted it down), and informed the appropriate department of the customer's request.

In most hotels, this is where the scenario ends.

But you're staying at a hotel where the general manager champions exceptional customer service in word and deed. He has, after careful thought, consideration, and collaboration with stakeholders, established the purpose of front desk agents' job role to be "Absolute Customer Satisfaction!" This is the employee's North Star influencing all of her actions and behaviors at work. It provides a simple context within which expectations can be conveyed and performance managed. That context is one question: "Is the customer *absolutely* satisfied?"

With this single highest priority informing her decisions,

1. she is exceedingly hospitable during the telephone conversation;
2. she confirms your room number (whether or not it appears on the digital display) in order to inspire confidence that your request was accurately noted;
3. she records the request on a digital or paper request log (which includes pertinent information such as the customer's name, room number, date, time, request, and request status);
4. she contacts the appropriate department to convey the request, confirming your name and room number, and seeks a follow-up call from a housekeeping representative when complete;
5. she remains vigilant by paying attention to the request log and the status of open requests;
6. she updates the request log after the room delivery is confirmed by a housekeeping staff member; and
7. she follows up with you directly to confirm delivery of the towels.

Because her single highest priority at work (Absolute Customer Satisfaction!) is informing her decisions, the front desk agent reflects the purpose of her job role in her actions and behaviors. In other words, she models job essence and seeks to

- express genuine interest
- display a sense of urgency
- confirm details (inspiring confidence)
- demonstrate care and concern
- be observant (paying attention to detail)
- follow up
- follow through
- accept personal responsibility
- take initiative
- deliver service heroics (when required)

Now, let's pose a slightly different scenario. What if the house-keeping staff fails to respond to the request quickly (or at all)? There are times in busy hotel operations when different departments are disproportionately affected by workloads, staffing levels, supply shortages, and other factors. At this point, the front desk agent has a variety of options that can include following up with the house-keeping staff to confirm the status of the request and even, with the consent of her supervisor, leaving her workstation to follow up in person. She may even exhibit service heroics by taking the initiative to deliver the towels to your room herself. More than executing job functions, the employee is going the extra mile to keep her focus on the purpose of her job role: Absolute Customer Satisfaction!

THE SWEET SPOT OF ENGAGEMENT

As Professor Dunning stated at the beginning of the chapter, many people are underperforming simply because they don't know that they could be doing better or what great performance looks like. Leaders owe it to their employees to provide them with these insights.

When employees possess adequate job knowledge and can demonstrate sufficient job skills, they are deemed competent to reliably execute job assignments. Being competent is a good thing — but it's not enough if you aspire to consistently engage employees and delight customers. To accomplish this, you must reveal the totality of your employees' job roles. When leaders lift the veil to expose the entire job role — job knowledge, job skills, and job purpose — they reveal the sweet spot where loyal customers and engaged employees flourish. In the next chapter you will be introduced to four questions to help you clarify employees' job purpose and other priorities so that conversations involving job purpose feel as natural and unrehearsed as those involving job functions.

Exercise

On the Venn diagram in figure 2, fill in what you see as your

- *job knowledge:* the learned facts, principles, concepts, and other pieces of information that are considered important in the performance of one's job role.
- *job skills:* the competencies one needs to perform tasks required of a particular job role; expertise or talent needed to do a job or task.
- *job purpose:* the reason a job role exists in support of organizational purpose. The job role's North Star. Importantly, this is not the *technical* reason a job role exists (e.g., an orthodontist's job role exists to straighten teeth). It is the *aspirational* reason a job role exists (e.g., an orthodontist's job role exists to create smiles or, more daring, instill confidence).

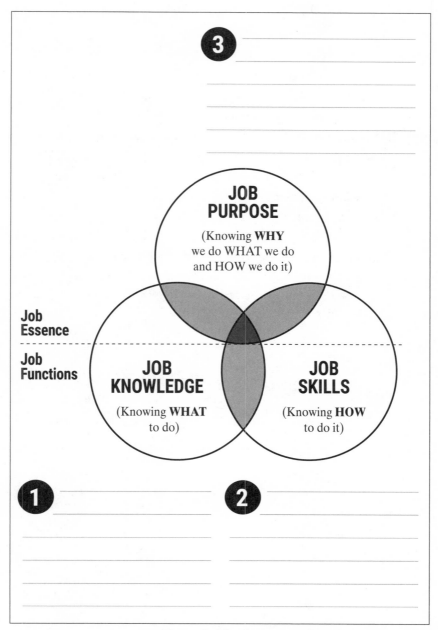

Figure 2: The Anatomy of a Job Role Exercise

Now may also be a good time to revisit your responses to questions 1 through 3 in chapter 1.

1. How close is the mission, vision, or purpose statement you recorded from memory to the actual statement that appears on your company's website?
2. When you audit your responses to question 2, what percentage of them pertain to job functions (duties and tasks associated with a job role) versus job essence (actions and behaviors that reflect job purpose)?
3. As you reconsider your response to question 3, how has your view of your employees' (or your own) single highest priority at work changed in light of the information contained in this chapter?

Part II

Connecting Job Functions to Job Purpose

3 | The Four Questions

Have you ever seen a Kihansi spray toad? I hadn't until I discovered them on an episode of *The Zoo* on Animal Planet. And if it weren't for the heroic conservation efforts of personnel at the Bronx Zoo in New York City, we wouldn't be able to see this species of toad in real life.

The Kihansi spray toad from Tanzania, Africa, was declared extinct in the wild in May 2009 due to the decimation of its environment —the unintended consequence of a hydroelectric dam that was built over the edge of a gorge, constraining a waterfall that had previously bathed the wetlands below in a constant, mistlike rain twenty-four hours a day. About nine months after the dam was activated, authorities realized the wetlands were drying up and the spray toads were in peril. The Tanzanian government partnered with specialists from the Bronx Zoo to collect the remaining toads for breeding purposes to expand their population. Bronx Zoo personnel collected 499 spray toads and split that group with conservationists at the Toledo Zoo to increase the odds of preserving the species because, at that point, those were all the spray toads in the world.[1]

Over the next decade, the Bronx Zoo developed a successful breeding program and the Kihansi spray toad was reintroduced to its native environment in Tanzania. It was the first time an amphibian had been reintroduced into its native habitat after being declared extinct in the wild.

The success of the Kihansi spray toad breeding program was not a happy accident. It was the result of a deliberate set of actions and behaviors that reflected the Bronx Zoo's purpose and values. According to zoo director Jim Breheny: "It's not enough to keep animals in exhibits just for people to look at. There has to be a higher purpose. And for us, it's conservation of species in the wild."[2]

This higher purpose is what informs the job purpose of every person on the Bronx Zoo staff. Avishai Shuter, who leads the toad's breeding program at the zoo shared: "These guys are absolutely my life's work. I view it as a personal challenge to keep the population here strong so that we can keep reintroducing back into the wild. And I want to make sure there will always be spray toads in the world because once they're gone, they're gone forever."[3]

In this quote, Mr. Shuter shares the purpose of his job role, his single highest priority at work. It matches the organizational purpose: "Conservation of species in the wild." He also gives us a peek into the values that guide his actions, behaviors, and decision-making: protection, collaboration, passion, and stewardship. These values manifest as the preservation of endangered species, cooperation with peers at the zoo and elsewhere to increase the odds of success of the breeding program, and enthusiasm for the toad's care and conservancy. His aspirational goal at work, it appears, is to preserve the Kihansi spray toad from extinction.

Part II, "Connecting Job Functions to Job Purpose," consists of chapters 3 through 5. The objective of chapter 3 is for the reader to be able to articulate employees' single highest priority at work. In the current chapter, I will pose four questions that will enable you to articulate job purpose, core values, purposeful actions and behaviors, and a purpose-driven aspirational goal. Your responses to these questions will prepare you to accomplish the objective of chapter

4, "Initiating the Revelation Conversation": to be able to recall the Revelation Conversation's framework in preparation to schedule and initiate the conversation with team members, connecting their daily job responsibilities to job purpose. The objective of chapter 5, "Aligning Actions and Behaviors with Purpose," is for readers to be able to identify purposeful actions and behaviors that will serve as leading indicators aimed at influencing lagging indicators—whether the achievement of departmental key performance indicators (KPIs) or progress toward the team's purpose and aspirational goal.

FROM ORGANIZATIONAL PURPOSE TO JOB PURPOSE

It may be useful here to distinguish between an organization's purpose and other ideals and priorities and those that are specific to a division, work group, or particular job role.

Organizational purpose is an organization's existential question, its reason for being. The organization's purpose or mission and other corporate ideals are generally articulated at corporate headquarters and then abdicated to the rest of the company, resulting in employees who tend to be less connected to them by virtue of the distance (both psychic and physical) separating them as well as the homogenous nature of these oftentimes broad and sweeping platitudes.

Jørgen Vig Knudstorp, former CEO of The Lego Group, said, "You really need to think hard about some simple questions, and those are: Why do you exist as a company? What is the really compelling reason why you exist? Of course, ultimately, you want to come up with something that's hugely relevant, and at the same time, very unique and really value-creating for other people. What's our philosophy, or doctrine? How can I say a few things about strategy and ways of behaving that then permeate the entire organization and allow me to empower and decentralize? The battle is not won in the CEO's office. It's won in the individual markets, and in meetings with customers."[4]

His quote reminds us that an effective organizational purpose applies to each business unit, no matter how far flung, and each employee, whether removed from customers at corporate headquarters or serving them directly on the front lines.

Job purpose narrows in on the aspirational reason a job role exists. It is the *why* associated with an employee's job-specific purpose. It is the employee's (and work group's) single highest priority at work, encapsulating its specific mission and purpose. It is aligned with and supports the organization's purpose, whatever it may be. It is also reflected in the aspirational goal of the employee, department, or work group. In contrast to organizational purpose, job purpose is defined locally and is specific to a particular job role within a department or work group. For these reasons, employees tend to be much more connected to job purpose—when they are made aware of it—which is why it is so important to reveal one's purpose at work and then make it real by connecting it to daily job duties.

In this chapter, we will begin the process of connecting organizational purpose to job purpose and linking job purpose to daily job responsibilities. This is how you as a supervisor, manager, or leader can make purpose tangible, proximate, and actionable in your real world of work, as opposed to its being something separate that is a part of your workday only during new-hire orientation, annual all-employee rallies, or annual performance reviews where the criterion "lives the vision" or similar is discussed. The first part of the process is answering the Four Questions (see figure 3).

THE FOUR QUESTIONS

1. What is my purpose at work?
2. What values guide my actions and behaviors at work?
3. What purposeful actions and behaviors do I exhibit at work?
4. What is my team's aspirational goal?

Every job role has a purpose, even if it is hidden from employee and customer view. The role of a formal purpose statement is to be able to articulate that purpose, connect it to employees' job roles, and leverage it to inspire employee engagement. The act of contemplating and responding to the Four Questions is designed to bring job purpose into the light, first for yourself as the leader, and then to help you enlighten your employees. This is how you give them something tangible to see and connect to—and customers something to sense and experience.

Answering these questions for yourself will connect you to your purpose at work (an afterthought for many) and prepares you to confidently initiate the Revelation Conversation with an employee. First, the questions help reacquaint you with your organization's existing mission, vision, or purpose statement(s) as well as its

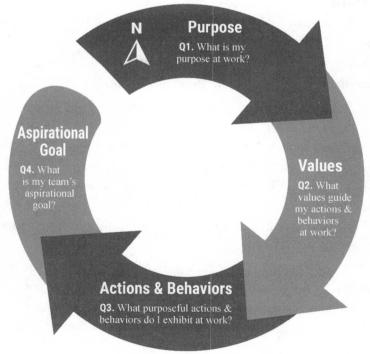

Figure 3: The Four Questions

corporate ideals, values, principles, pillars, or guideposts.* You must be fluent in these corporate ideals if you expect to have any credibility connecting employees' job duties and tasks to job purpose. Second, they help you develop your own understanding of how core organizational values can shape behavior, decision-making, and the development of team goals and aspirations. Third, they help you get your own house in order. You must be able to articulate your own job purpose and model the values, actions, and behaviors that support it before you ask the same of your employees. That is why I recommend first answering these questions for yourself before exploring what the answers might be for any of your employees. It is true that there will be overlap in the responses as they apply to your role and the roles of those whom you supervise, manage, or lead, and with whom you work as peers. And, in some cases, the responses will be identical.

If you work for a large company, chances are you already have an authentic, well-worded mission, vision, or purpose statement, and an articulated set of core values. There are advantages and disadvantages to this. It's useful to have the organizational purpose and values crystallized. Assuming these corporate ideals are credible and relevant, much of the work in answering the questions will have been done for you. Your job, then, is to adapt these corporate-level ideals to your local workplace and make them applicable to your employees' job roles and work groups. In some cases, as with the Bronx Zoo illustration, the organizational purpose and your (or your employees') job-specific purpose may even be one and the same. Great! You can check off question 1 and, if core values exist, perhaps question 2.

The disadvantage, however, to having these polished statements and values available as turnkey corporate ideals is that you can fill in those answers without putting a lot of original thought into them. When you have to come up with your own answers—for yourself

---

* Companies use a variety of creative terms to capture the essence of their history, character, and culture.

and for your employees—you reinforce the connections between job purpose, core values, purposeful actions and behaviors, and the team's aspirational goal. If your company does not have a defined purpose statement and a set of core values teed up, answering the Four Questions will be more time-intensive, but the process may be more rewarding. You will likely need to do more discovery. This may take the form of questioning the founder or long-term employees to learn the company's history, uncover its origin story, and begin to knit a rich tapestry of its past. You will need to learn about the company's products, services, triumphs, setbacks, and the decisions that led to them. You will be challenged to do the contemplative thinking required to remove layers of organizational veneer to access what your company stands for beneath the surface. Each of these valuable pieces of information will help lead you to the most meaningful answers to the Four Questions.

1. What is my purpose at work?

As proposed in chapter 1, the life purpose of the great majority of employees (for the relative few who have articulated one) is often separate and distinct from their purpose at work. In reality, a company has no control over the life purpose of its employees. But a company has complete control over if, when, and how it articulates job purpose for its employees. Even so, of the companies that do articulate a coherent purpose, most underutilize it. As Carol Cone reported, PwC found that "79 percent of business leaders believe that purpose is central to success. Despite this, less than half of employees know what their organization stands for and what makes it different."[5]

Too often, corporate mission, vision, and purpose statements, along with core values, principles, and tenets, are carefully crafted, added to the company website, inserted in the employee handbook, and framed behind a pane of glass and mounted in the executive corridor. Initially trumpeted through a corporate campaign, emblazoned on buttons, koozies, and other swag, it is there that these commitments to customers and high ideals languish and fade into obscurity. These corporate declarations are isolated and removed from employees' daily job roles and, as a result, have little to no effect on their actions and behaviors or the experience of customers.

A job role's purpose should support the overall organizational purpose *and* be specific to the unique role-based contributions made by the employee or work group. But there is a danger in articulating a job purpose that is overly focused on job functions. In doing so, the aspirational quality of the job role's purpose is stamped out in favor of a more tactical purpose. You will know that has been done when the job purpose reads more like a bullet point on a job description than an ambitious pursuit. My litmus test to determine the effectiveness of a job purpose is whether it can be quantified. If it can, it's not ready.

For example, you might want to articulate a hotel housekeeper's job purpose as "to provide a clean guest room" or a hotel laundry attendant's job role as "to provide clean towels and bed linens." Each of these job purpose statements is lacking. Both sound like formal job responsibilities and can easily be measured, quantified, and ranked. A hotel's housekeeping department uses a variety of objective evaluations to assess the cleanliness of a guest room. The same is true of its laundry operations, whose quality is increasingly verified by an independent third-party certification body.

Instead, leaders and managers should ask the question *why* multiple times to push past the core deliverable (*What* do we produce and *how* do we produce it?) to the true purpose of the job role (*Why* do we produce it?).

Using the hotel housekeeper example, ask a follow-up question, such as, "Why do we provide guests with a clean room?"

The answer might be, "To meet their expectations." You are now a step closer to the job purpose.

Ask again, "Why do we want to meet guests' expectations?"

Perhaps, "To increase their intent to recommend our hotel to others."

And again, "Why do we want to increase their intent to recommend our hotel to others?"

Maybe, "Because the 'intent to recommend' question on our customer satisfaction survey is correlated with guest loyalty."

So, "Why is guest loyalty important?"

And, finally, "Because our loyal guests are responsible for 80–90 percent of the positive word of mouth about our hotel, are less price sensitive, and have higher return and repurchase rates. All of these behaviors contribute to our success."

By following a similar sequence of questions to get at the deeper, underlying purpose of the housekeeper's job role, you have now discovered that her purpose is not to provide a clean room. Rather, it is to create a loyal customer.

Now, ask yourself, "How will a housekeeper behave differently if she is made aware that the purpose of her job role, her single highest priority at work, is not merely to provide a clean room (as outlined in her job description and detailed in her supervisor's inspection form) but to create a loyal customer?"

In addition to cleaning the room, will she

- check the batteries in the TV remote?
- verify that the time on the digital clock is correct?
- ensure that the alarm set by the previous guest has been deactivated?
- look underneath the bed to make sure there is no evidence of a previous guest?
- wrap a phone charging cord and bind it with a complimentary silicone clip (as is done by the professional housekeeping staff at The Broadmoor hotel and resort in Colorado Springs, Colorado)?
- neatly place the bathroom toiletries on a washcloth?

- take steps to report any maintenance issues that she observes?
- double-check the room's thermostat to confirm its setting?
- leave a personalized note?

These actions and behaviors, and many others, are correlated with increased guest satisfaction, which is correlated with guest loyalty, which is correlated with the above loyalty behaviors (positive word of mouth, less price sensitivity, and higher return and repurchase rates). This is how you begin to make connections between an employee's job functions (duties and tasks) and the purpose of their job role. It activates job purpose. It makes work compelling and meaningful, and drives people to do their best work.

On occasion, you can make an argument for the employee's job purpose matching the organization's purpose. At the end of this section, you'll find a list of successful companies that do this well. One very good example is the hotel company Hyatt. Its organizational purpose statement reads: "To care for people so they can be their best." This applies to everyone's job role, whether they are a housekeeper, laundry attendant, front desk agent, restaurant server, maintenance engineer, human resources director, or general manager. It does not read like a staid job responsibility. It is aspirational, not tactical. As a result, it cannot be quantified in the same way you could rate the cleanliness of a hotel room or pillowcase.

Other times, the organization's sweeping purpose statement will be less relevant to the daily job responsibilities of an employee. Take the purpose statement of the supermarket conglomerate Kroger: "To feed the human spirit." Although noble, it is rather lofty and abstract and doesn't pertain directly to the job role of, say, an employee whose responsibilities include sacking groceries, bringing carts inside the store from the parking lot, sweeping the floor, and cleaning the public restrooms. If I were this employee's supervisor, I would find it awkward to cajole him into cleaning a public restroom or mopping up a spill on aisle 10 by championing the job purpose: "Feed the human spirit, Todd!"

In this case, it's important to honor the organization's purpose while adapting the job role's purpose to one that is relevant to the job role and will resonate with the employee. A closer look at Kroger's corporate ideals reveals that this purpose is meant to accomplish its pledge "to be friendly and caring, provide everything fresh, to uplift every way, and improve every day."[6] Now we have something to work with.

I may submit that this employee's job purpose, his single highest priority at work, is *to provide everything fresh*. As his supervisor, I might set the aspirational goal of "Provide everything fresh!" With that mantra as the standard, a dirty public restroom or allowing a spill on aisle 10 to linger is unacceptable. It puts a stake in the ground. It is Kroger's line in the sand that no one dares breach. Doing so would not be tolerated by employees who have committed to provide everything fresh.

It's important, though, to not get hung up on definitions. Many overarching organizational purposes make great job purposes, as Hyatt's organizational purpose demonstrates. Also, many mission statements read like purpose statements. That's okay. These organizations do not have to manufacture a purpose statement to comply with a silly rule that "mission statements are not purpose statements."

To appease the organizational development lexicon police (ODLP), I will say that, generally speaking, vision statements tend to have a longer time horizon than mission statements. Oftentimes, but not always, vision statements will contain *to be*, a reference to the organization's desired future state. Meanwhile, purpose statements tend to be more existential, literally describing the reason an organization exists.

I thought about including a comprehensive set of definitions with examples to distinguish between these types of statements (mission, vision, and purpose) but decided against it. Whether or not you call a statement by the right name doesn't matter. What's more important is that *you can recall your organization's statement*, regardless of whether it's labeled as a mission, vision, or purpose statement (or something else, like a creed, motto, or mantra), and that leaders at all levels of the organization know it, embrace it, exude it, model it, communicate it, champion it, and connect it to employees' daily job responsibilities.

WHAT'S IN A NAME?

Here's a fun quiz that highlights the fact that what you call your organization's mission, vision, or purpose statement isn't nearly as important as what you do with it.

Figures 4 and 5 contain random listings of well-known companies and their guiding statements. In the column on the right, indicate whether you think each statement describes a mission (M), vision (V), or purpose (P) statement.

Here's the scoring scale:

32–35 = A; 28–31 = B; 25–27 = C; 21–24 = D.

So how did you do?

I suspect you scored better on the last test you took, whether at the DMV or the eye doctor. But don't fret. This may be one of the least consequential tests you will take. While it's true that a purpose statement describes the reason an organization exists, many published and credible mission and vision statements (from sophisticated, multibillion-dollar companies) do exactly the same thing (I guess no one told those companies they were doing it all wrong). But if we can't tell the difference between what qualifies as a mission, vision, or purpose statement, then does it really matter what we call it?

I think not. The critical piece is that, regardless of what you call it, you can *recall* it. It must be more than website candy, a clever turn of phrase, or a slick corporate poster.

Company	Statement	Mission, Vision, or Purpose?
Tesla	To accelerate the world's transition to sustainable energy.	
TED	Spread ideas.	
LinkedIn	To connect the world's professionals to make them more productive and successful.	
Virgin Atlantic	To embrace the human spirit and let it fly.	
Whole Foods Market	To nourish people and the planet.	
PayPal	To build the web's most convenient, secure, cost-effective payment solution.	
Amazon	To be Earth's most customer-centric company, Earth's best employer, and Earth's safest place to work.	
Ford Motor Company	To help build a better world, where every person is free to move and pursue their dreams.	
Asana	To help humanity thrive by enabling the world's teams to work together effortlessly.	
Patagonia	We're in business to save our home planet.	
General Motors	A world with zero crashes, zero emissions, and zero congestion.	
Harley-Davidson	Building our legend and leading our industry through innovation, evolution, and emotion.	
The Walt Disney Company	To entertain, inform, and inspire people around the globe through the power of unparalleled storytelling, reflecting the iconic brands, creative minds, and innovative technologies that make ours the world's premier entertainment company.	
Google	To organize the world's information and make it universally accessible and useful.	
IKEA	To create a better everyday life for the many people—for customers, but also for our coworkers and the people who work at our suppliers.	
Microsoft	To empower every person and every organization on the planet to achieve more.	
Sony Corporation	To be a company that inspires and fulfills your curiosity.	
Uber	We ignite opportunity by setting the world in motion.	

Figure 4: Mission, Vision, or Purpose Quiz (part 1)

Company	Statement	Mission, Vision, or Purpose?
OXFAM	To help create lasting solutions to the injustice of poverty.	
McDonald's	To make delicious feel-good moments easy for everyone.	
Target	The promise of surprises, fun, ease, and inspiration at every turn, no matter when, where, or how you shop.	
Starbucks	To inspire and nurture the human spirit—one person, one cup, and one neighborhood at a time.	
Warby Parker	To inspire and impact the world with vision, purpose, and style.	
Zappos	To live and deliver WOW.	
Charles Schwab	To champion every client's goals with passion and integrity.	
Nike	Bring inspiration and innovation to every athlete in the world.	
Alzheimer's Association	A world without Alzheimer's.	
Life is Good	To spread the power of optimism.	
United Airlines	Connecting people. Uniting the world.	
Kiva	To expand financial access to help underserved communities thrive.	
Southwest Airlines	To be the world's most loved, most efficient, and most profitable airline.	
Facebook	Give people the power to build community and bring the world closer together.	
Target	To help all families discover the joy of everyday life.	
DICK'S Sporting Goods	We create an inclusive environment where passionate, skilled, and diverse teammates thrive. We create and build leading brands that serve and inspire athletes. We deliver shareholder value through growth and relentless improvement. We make a lasting impact on communities through sport.	
General Mills	To make food the world loves.	

Figure 5: Mission, Vision, or Purpose Quiz (part 2)

Figure 7, the answer key, is at the end of this chapter. Good luck!

When I ask managers, across industries, to write down their organization's purpose statement, and then compare their submissions with the version trumpeted on the company website, on average, only 6 percent of managers can accurately cite it. This points to a dissonance between what companies say and do relative to organizational purpose. One study found that while 76 percent of the marketing heads surveyed were of the belief that their organization had a defined sense of purpose, only a paltry one in ten could produce a corporate purpose statement and a plan to back up these beliefs.[7] Clearly, there is an opportunity to enlighten management about the significance of organizational purpose and, once articulated, how to leverage it to achieve a purposeful advantage.

When I ask these same managers to describe their employees' job roles, on average, 85 percent of the descriptions pertain to executing job functions. The remaining 15 percent relate to job essence, the actions and behaviors that reflect job purpose. Because this is the common lens through which managers view employees' job roles and evaluate their performance, it is no surprise that when asked, employees themselves overwhelmingly define their job roles in terms of job functions with little or no reference to job essence.

There are, however, exceptions. A client organization, a major automotive parts retailer, is intentional about aligning its retail store clerks with its core values of loyalty, integrity, and devotion by reframing their job role; instead of retail clerks, they are consultative advisers. This means that store employees who used to view their job role as executing retail transactions now see themselves as consultants who have the long-term best interest of the customer and vehicle in mind. Now, when customers bring an automotive part up to the counter to pay, instead of blindly ringing it up, the employee might ask one or more questions to verify that the customer has the correct part and is aware of the scope of the repair.

For example, if a customer asks about purchasing brake pads and rotors for an older vehicle, mentioning that they heard they can save a lot of money by doing the repair themselves, store employees have been trained to assess the customer's experience with this type of repair. If they prove to be a novice, the employee will recommend that the customer leave one side of the brake assembly intact to be viewed for comparison while the other side is rebuilt. The employee is also trained to provide an overview of the repair and the tools and other products required, including brake cleaner, brake fluid, and caliper lube.

By acting as a consultant, the employee provides a helpful tip and may eliminate the need for the customer to make a second trip to the store to purchase a tool or other product required to complete the repair.

Many people spend the majority of their waking hours at work, so being intentional about revealing job purpose, besides elevating customer service quality, can enable more meaningful work experiences and more fulfilling work environments.

WHEN JOB PURPOSE AND ORGANIZATIONAL PURPOSE ALIGN

In articulating the purpose of a job role, you need to make sure that it supports the overall organizational purpose and that it is relevant to the unique role-based contributions made by the employee. Sometimes, these two purposes are so aligned that they are one and the same, as with the Disneyland (chapter 2), Bronx Zoo, and Hyatt examples. Below is a list of broad, sweeping organizational purpose statements taken directly from company websites. They apply universally across the company, regardless of region, division, department, or job role.

- To empower people to stay a step ahead in life and in business (ING financial services)
- Creating better days and a place at the table for everyone through our trusted food brands (Kellogg Company)
- To make your world a safer place (IAG Limited)
- To make an impact that matters (Deloitte)
- To develop leaders of character dedicated to serving the greater good (Texas A&M University)
- To build trust in society and solve important problems (PwC)
- Every day, we help unite the world by connecting people to the moments that matter most (United Airlines)
- To help build a better world, where every person is free to move and pursue their dreams (Ford Motor Company)
- Cultivating coffee as an art to grow the best in each of us (Nespresso)
- To create happiness by providing the finest in entertainment for people of all ages, everywhere (The Walt Disney Company)
- Caring for people so they can be their best (Hyatt)

2. What values guide my actions and behaviors at work?

I know of a company that made a job offer to a candidate who subsequently gave two weeks' notice to his current employer. Within those two weeks, President Trump declared COVID-19 a national emergency and the hiring firm shuttered its four offices in the US and Canada to allow its staff to work remotely while absorbing the loss of a dozen retainer clients. The manager felt compelled under the circumstances to rescind the job offer. But before that action was taken, the firm's chairman directed him to honor the original offer.

Some might question the wisdom of this decision given the uncertainty of an economy where furloughs, layoffs, and record jobless claims dominated the headlines. The reason lay in one of the firm's core values: keep promises. This means that employees keep their word and foster a reputation for dependability. It's true that in the short term the firm could have reduced its payroll costs by rescinding the job offer. But consider the long-term benefits derived from upholding corporate values even when it's inconvenient, costly, or seemingly justifiable to subvert them.

Imagine the effect on the hiring manager who experienced, first-hand, the integrity of the company chairman. And think about the potential criticism from the jilted job applicant that was avoided and the future contributions he may make to the firm. And what about current employees who take their cues from leadership? How has this action affected their morale, engagement levels, productivity, and pride in working for their employer? These are all rhetorical questions for now, but they will ultimately be answered in engagement surveys, utilization reports, and turnover analysis.

A company's core values are the fundamental beliefs, ideals, or practices that inform company decisions and guide behavior. Too often, however, these foundational values appear as an aspirational list on a company's *About* webpage or logoed coffee mug but have little to do with day-to-day decision-making. This is why it's important to think deeply about how these core values should trickle down to a division, work group, or particular job role. While there will likely be significant if not complete overlap with the organization's overarching values, reflecting on them provides you with the opportunity to identify which are most important to your team or to redefine certain values in a way that resonates with the team's specific function or purpose. And once you can articulate a set of job-specific values for your employees, then these values can serve as a touchstone for their behavior and decision-making. As Roy Disney of The Walt Disney Company said, "When your values are clear to you, making decisions becomes easier."[8]

Take pharmaceutical giant Pfizer, maker of the first-to-market COVID-19 vaccine as an example. Pfizer CEO Albert Bourla was asked whether the rapid development of a vaccine in 2020 could be characterized as a miracle.

His response: "I want to make something very, very clear. [It] was not luck. [It] was very deliberate. It was the result of hundreds of decisions that had to be made along the way. . . . We were successful, not lucky."[9]

Now, let's drill down further to see how Pfizer's values are reflected in a specific working group. The company's organizational purpose is *to deliver breakthroughs that change patients' lives*. Like Disneyland, the Bronx Zoo, and Hyatt, Pfizer's organizational purpose may also serve as the purpose of the job role across functions. Below is the ambitious set of values Pfizer has articulated to support this purpose:

- *Courage.* Breakthroughs start by challenging convention, especially in the face of uncertainty or adversity. This happens when we think big, speak up, and are decisive.
- *Excellence.* We can change patients' lives only when we perform at our best together. This happens when we focus on what matters, agree who does what, and measure our outcomes.
- *Equity.* We believe that every person deserves to be seen, heard, and cared for. This happens when we are inclusive, act with integrity, and reduce health care disparities.
- *Joy.* We give ourselves to our work, but it also gives to us. We find joy when we take pride, recognize one another, and have fun.[10]

The way that Pfizer presents its core values is instructive. Rather than simply compiling a set of imitative values that did not, by themselves, differentiate Pfizer from other pharmaceutical companies, it added context by expanding each word into a statement. And it further deciphered each one by specifying the desired behaviors that will reflect the value in action.

As the leadership author Patrick Lencioni observed, "55 percent of all Fortune 100 companies claim integrity is a core value, 49 percent espouse customer satisfaction, and 40 percent tout teamwork. While these are inarguably good qualities, such terms hardly provide a distinct blueprint for employee behavior. Cookie-cutter values don't set a company apart from competitors; they make it fade into the crowd."[11]

As depicted in figure 6, Pfizer recognized that its chosen values were somewhat abstract as is and that there was an opportunity to add context with an explanatory statement and describe what those values in action would look like.

Pfizer employees' job functions vary depending on job role, so their purpose and values are reflected in different ways. For example, those charged with pricing the COVID-19 vaccine (a job function), priced it at the cost of distributing it to low-income

Values	Statements	Behaviors
Courage	Breakthroughs start by challenging convention, especially in the face of uncertainty or adversity.	This happens when we think big, speak up, and are decisive.
Excellence	We can change patients' lives only when we perform at our best together.	This happens when we focus on what matters, agree who does what, and measure our outcomes.
Equity	We believe that every person deserves to be seen, heard, and cared for.	This happens when we are inclusive, act with integrity, and reduce health care disparities.
Joy	We give ourselves to our work, but it also gives to us.	We find joy when we take pride, recognize one another, and have fun.

Figure 6: Values, Statements, and Behaviors

countries.[12] This decision not only supports its purpose—to deliver breakthroughs that change patients' lives—but also reflects its value of *equity* by reducing health care disparities and its value of *courage* by challenging convention. So, here's the relationship between purpose and values: Pfizer would not have been able to fulfill its purpose of delivering breakthroughs and changing patients' lives if the company had priced the vaccine so high that lower-income countries could not afford it. To make good on its purpose, Pfizer needed a purpose- and values-driven pricing model.*

3. What purposeful actions and behaviors do I exhibit at work?

After you have uncovered the purpose of the job role and its associated core values (expanding them into statements and labeling what they look like in action), put thought into the specific actions and behaviors that will *actuate* job purpose and core values.

To revisit the Pfizer example, its organizational purpose (which may also serve as the purpose of the job role across functions) is *to deliver breakthroughs that change patients' lives*. And one of its values is *equity*. This value was expanded into a value statement in figure 6 that added context and illustrated, rather broadly, what the value looks like in practice.

In addressing question 3, examine what you can do in your area of responsibility, in terms of planned, rehearsed actions and recommended behaviors that will bring your job purpose and core values to life. In the Pfizer example, we looked at the decision to price the COVID-19 vaccine at cost for low-income countries. If, as a leadership team member at Pfizer, pharmaceutical pricing falls within your area of responsibility, then you might label the behavior "Consider the effects of product pricing on health care disparities in the markets

---

* Pfizer will likely not maintain pandemic-era pricing for its vaccine as the world emerges from the crisis and prices are negotiated by insurance companies rather than linked to the government preorders of 2020, during the height of the emergency.

we serve" and the action "Develop a purpose- and values-driven pricing model for the markets we serve."

To revisit the Disneyland example, its founding organizational purpose (which may also serve as the purpose of the job role across functions) is *to create happiness for others*. And one of its core values is *quality*. We saw this value reflected in the behavior of *paying attention to detail* and the action of instituting a *hypervigilant maintenance program* in the daily restoration of the horse-head hitching posts lining Main Street U.S.A. at Disneyland.

And to revisit the Kroger example, its organizational purpose *to feed the human spirit* didn't naturally apply to the daily job duties of the store employee responsible for the cleanup on aisle 10, so it was adapted to *provide everything fresh* as the purpose of the job role. This adaptation was not arbitrary. It was based on Kroger's commitment *to be friendly and caring, provide everything fresh, to uplift every way, and improve every day*. One of Kroger's values is *integrity*. I've heard integrity defined as the integration of principles—the fundamental truths that serve as the foundation of a belief system. When you integrate, or combine, the core values and principles that gird your belief system into a universal whole, you manifest organizational culture.

At Kroger, the value of integrity is evident in the employee's *responsiveness* to the cleanup on aisle 10 and the *quality* with which the spill is removed and the aisle's freshness is restored. Incidentally, another one of Kroger's core values is *safety*. You can immediately see the link between employees' responsiveness to cleanups and the value of safety by eliminating the threat of a slip and fall as quickly as possible.

A word of caution is needed here: question 3 is the question most likely to be ignored or left to chance. There is a tendency among leaders to believe that once they have articulated a mission, vision, or purpose statement and a set of core values, they are done. The popular assumption is that the guiding statements and values will somehow permeate the organization and influence employee behavior on their own, apart from any additional effort by leadership. This is incorrect. Energy flows where attention goes. Be highly attentive to the actions and behaviors that will bring your organizational and job role's purpose and core values to the forefront of employees' day-to-day job responsibilities—their real world of work.

4. What is my team's aspirational goal?

Chouinard Equipment was a mountain climbing gear company cofounded by Yvon Chouinard in 1965. By 1970, it had become the largest supplier of climbing hardware in the US. Its products included pitons, steel spikes that are driven into a crack or seam in the rock surface to support climbers. The same fragile cracks have had to endure the repeated hammering of pitons during both placement and removal, disfiguring landforms across the nation.[13]

As pressure from interest groups mounted, Mr. Chouinard transitioned from the environmentally destructive iron pitons to aluminum chocks that could be wedged by hand rather than hammered in and out of surface cracks. This would be one of the first environmentally conscious decisions made by the company that would later become Patagonia.[14]

Since 1973, Patagonia has been at the leading edge of environmental activism, sustainable supply chains, and advocacy for public lands and the outdoors. Its mission has long been "Build the best product, cause no unnecessary harm, use business to inspire and implement solutions to the environmental crisis."[15] In addition to eco-friendly business practices linked to sourcing and manufacturing, Patagonia contributes a self-imposed Earth tax, 1 percent of its annual net revenue, to grassroots environmental causes.[16] Even so, Mr. Chouinard, now in his eighties, felt as if the company's efforts were being marginalized by the broad scope of its mission.

So, in 2018, Patagonia revised its mission statement to "Patagonia is in business to save our home planet."[17] In doing so, it narrowed its team's focus by emphasizing its ultimate goal.

Similarly, organizations can narrow employees' focus, spur performance, and reinforce commitment by establishing an aspirational goal. When this goal is made clear to all stakeholders, it can become a source of guidance, ambition, and inspiration.

Many organizational leaders focus on tactical goals related to job functions or KPIs while relegating purpose to feel-good sentiment emblazoned on corporate tchotchkes and occasionally mentioned in the CEO's public remarks and corporate press releases. Or they ignore purpose altogether. But aspirational goals—those imbued with a higher purpose—are much more effective at focusing employees' attention and harnessing a team's collective efforts.

An aspirational goal describes a desired eventuality. It speaks to the pursuit of an ideal future state or destination. And for meaningful progress to be made toward this goal, it must be tied to employees' job purpose. This way, their collective actions, behaviors, and decisions will all facilitate progression toward that goal. Unlike tactical goals that dispassionately guide the execution of job functions, an aspirational goal can be audacious, extravagant, and daring. The goal should have the capacity to inspire esprit de corps, a feeling of pride, fellowship, and common loyalty, among employees.

As we saw in the examples of Pfizer, Disneyland, and Kroger, this commitment will spur employees to reflect core values in decision-making, pay attention to detail, display a sense of urgency, and demonstrate a willingness to expend discretionary effort in other ways.

THE NEXT BIG STEP

Once you have answered the Four Questions, you are now equipped to initiate the Revelation Conversation. A word of caution: this is the point where many well-intentioned professionals who invest the time to respond to these important questions pause and return their attention to job functions, which are familiar, proximate, and easy to measure. This is where I encourage you to step out of your safe space, to own your responsibility for fostering engaged employees, and to do the work to initiate your first Revelation Conversation, as we'll discuss in the next chapter.

Exercise

QUESTION 1: WHAT IS MY PURPOSE AT WORK?

Why does my job role exist? What is my single highest priority at work?

In arriving at the purpose of a job role, it's beneficial to explore the organization's overarching purpose and consider how it should be reflected in the job role. Start with the reason for your organization's existence. Recognize that an organizational purpose exists regardless of whether leadership chooses to articulate it, communicate it to all employees, and connect it to employees' job roles. It's also important to remember that the organizational and job purposes are aspirational. The job purpose is not the technical reason a job role exists. It reflects the role's single highest priority. The job purpose is the job role's North Star.

Question 1: What is my purpose at work?

_____

_____

_____

_____

_____

_____

QUESTION 2: WHAT VALUES GUIDE MY ACTIONS AND BEHAVIORS AT WORK?

On what do I base my decision-making? As shown by the company that stood by a job offer it had made in the weeks leading up to the

COVID-19 national emergency, an immutable set of values serves as a touchstone for decision-making. It's true that when values are clear, decisions are easy.

In arriving at the job-specific values that inform your actions and behaviors at work, it's beneficial to explore the relationship between the organization's core values and those of the job role. Organizational values should support both organizational purpose and job purpose by informing and guiding employee behavior at all levels.

Question 2: What values guide my actions and behaviors at work?

_____

_____

_____

_____

_____

_____

QUESTION 3: WHAT PURPOSEFUL ACTIONS AND BEHAVIORS DO I EXHIBIT AT WORK?

If purpose merely hangs from the wall in the form of a poster and values reside only on a screen saver or coffee mug, then they are of little day-to-day benefit to the organization. By identifying purpose-driven actions and behaviors in advance and leveraging values-driven decision-making in real time, companies can manifest their purpose in the products, services, and experiences they deliver to each of their customer groups, whether internal or external to the organization.

Question 3: What purposeful actions and behaviors do I exhibit at work?

_____

_____

_____

_____

_____

_____

QUESTION 4: WHAT IS MY TEAM'S ASPIRATIONAL GOAL?

What ideal future state does my team envision?

An aspirational goal speaks to the pursuit of an ideal future state or destination. Unlike tactical goals that dispassionately guide the execution of job functions, an aspirational goal can be excessively grand or ambitious—almost over the top.

Aspirational goals are effective at focusing employees' attention and harnessing a team's collective efforts. But for meaningful progress to be made toward these types of goals, they must be linked to an employee's and work group's job purpose. In that way, their actions, behaviors, and decisions all contribute toward that goal.

Question 4: What is my team's aspirational goal?

_____

_____

_____

_____

_____

_____

ANSWER KEY									
Tesla	M	Ford Motor Company	P	IKEA	V	Starbucks	M	United Airlines	P
TED	M	Asana	M	Microsoft	M	Warby Parker	M	Kiva	M
LinkedIn	M	Patagonia	M	Sony Corporation	M	Zappos	P	Southwest Airlines	V
Virgin Atlantic	P	General Motors	V	Uber	M	Charles Schwab	P	Facebook	M
Whole Foods Market	P	Harley-Davidson	V	OXFAM	P	Nike	M	Target	P
PayPal	M	The Walt Disney Company	M	McDonald's	M	Alzheimer's Association	V	DICK'S Sporting Goods	M
Amazon	M	Google	M	Target	M	Life is Good	M	General Mills	P

Figure 7: Quiz Answer Key

Here's the scoring scale: 32–35 = A; 28–31 = B; 25–27 = C; 21–24 = D

4 | Initiating the Revelation Conversation

hree years ago, I joined several colleagues for dinner at a hotel in downtown Philadelphia. A colleague who had traveled in from St. Louis was looking forward to ordering a Philly cheesesteak during his one night in town. When he didn't spot it on the menu, he asked the waiter if the restaurant served the city's signature sandwich and was dismayed to learn that it was served for lunch but not dinner.

Now this was a sophisticated urban hotel with a professional full-service kitchen. It's not beyond the realm of possibility to think that the chef, whose kitchen stocked flank steak, onions, green bell peppers, provolone cheese, and hoagie rolls, could surprise and delight my colleague by making an exception and crafting a delicious Philly cheesesteak for him. Had this occurred, it would have left a lasting impression and inspired a positive story to share.

As you might imagine, the lodging company that manages this hotel has a lofty mission statement that exalts the guest and trumpets customer delight. The only problem is that our experience did not reflect those ideals at all. Rather than explore possibilities, our server seemed indifferent toward my colleague's disappointment.

(Keep in mind that his request was hardly unreasonable. He was simply trying to order a Philly cheesesteak in Philadelphia.)

It's no secret that competent servers are knowledgeable about menu items, specials, prices, and food ingredients that may affect dietary restrictions. They must also be skillful in the way they operate the point of sale (POS) system, carry a tray, deliver and clear tableware, and serve beverages. Being competent will suffice if the goal is to reliably execute assigned transactions. But if the goal is fully engaged employees exhibiting purposeful actions and behaviors, then competency is not enough.

Let's say we identified the employee's job purpose as "to surprise and delight guests." Then, they should be exuding "surprise and delight" in their attitude, demeanor, and individual flair. They should be honoring the company culture by initiating surprising and delightful acts that will expand company lore while reinforcing the alignment between the experience the company promises and the one its employees deliver. They should be reflecting the ideals inherent in the corporate mission statement. They should be upholding performance standards designed to incorporate purposeful actions and behaviors *into* job functions to operationalize "surprise and delight."

Importantly, I did not blame the server in the above scenario for our less-than-delightful experience. When something goes wrong, it's easiest to look for and assign blame to the person right in front of you. But tempting as it is to fault the server, rarely are frontline service providers the source of poor customer service quality. More likely, the root cause is having an incomplete view of their job role and being unaware of their purpose at work. And it's the responsibility of their immediate supervisor to reveal the total job role and demonstrate how it links to job purpose.

BLAME THE PROCESS, NOT THE PERSON

Years ago, I met the renowned statistician and Edwards Deming protégé Brian Joiner at his quality institute in Madison, Wisconsin.

In an environment presumably focused on statistical process controls, thresholds, and compliance, Dr. Joiner was compassionate in largely absolving workers as the primary source of variation in a system or process. An oft-repeated mantra of his was "blame the process, not the person."

When supervisors ask themselves, "How did the process allow this to happen?" and then thoughtfully examine the related sequence of events that may have contributed to an unsatisfactory result, a new picture often emerges. Many processes (selection, onboarding, department training, performance management, etc.) contributed to the quality of the service experience that we received from our server. Among them was the server's incomplete view of his job role. As was discussed in chapter 2, most supervisors define the totality of employees' job roles in terms of job functions, their duties and tasks. In such a work environment, a server's competency is determined by the extent to which he possesses adequate job knowledge and demonstrates sufficient job skills. If he meets the minimum requirements for each, then he is deemed competent or capable to reliably execute job assignments.

But this view of the employee's job role is lacking. Although it recognizes the importance of job knowledge and skills, it disregards job purpose, his single highest priority at work, which might be to surprise and delight guests, add value during each interaction, or create promoters of the hotel's restaurant. Before finding fault with our server, his supervisor must first consider if he has been made aware of the purpose of his job role and how his daily job responsibilities link to it. If not, then the Revelation Conversation can help him to accomplish this.

WHAT IS THE REVELATION CONVERSATION?

The Revelation Conversation is a framework for revealing to your employees the *why* behind their job roles and how that *why* should be reflected in their actions and behaviors while executing their job assignments. There are three primary objectives of the Revelation Conversation:

- to reveal the total job role: job knowledge (the *what*), job skills (the *how*), and job purpose (the *why*)
- to connect job functions to job purpose, making purpose a tangible part of employees' real world of work
- to inspire greater employee engagement

If I were managing the Philadelphia restaurant server in our example, I would make it a priority to initiate the Revelation Conversation. My first responsibility would be to educate myself. Can I, as the manager, confidently and accurately articulate the purpose of his job role? If not, I need to reflect on the Four Questions posed in chapter 3 and access resources to help me locate this information, such as the corporate website, human resources, and my own supervisor.

Let's say that I discover that the purpose of his job role is, in fact, to surprise and delight our guests. Next, I would approach him one-on-one and pose this question: "Would you describe for me, from your perspective, your job role—what your job entails?"

Most likely he will provide a list dominated by job functions. In my experience, there is rarely any mention of job purpose or actions and behaviors that reflect that purpose.

Accepting responsibility for the incomplete view of his job role, I would respond, "That's an impressive list of job responsibilities. All of those things are important and necessary. But it sounds like I haven't fully explained your job role to you. Those job functions are only one dimension of your job role. The other dimension is job essence."

"What is job essence?" he'll ask.

"Job essence is the most significant aspect of your job role. It is the actions and behaviors that reflect your job purpose, your single highest priority at work."

"What's my single highest priority?"

"Your single highest priority at work is to surprise and delight guests."

"Besides what I'm already doing, what else can I do?"

The conversation that follows might just be the most valuable use of your time at work.

Revelation Conversations are a great opportunity to reveal and reinforce

- job purpose
- company culture
- corporate ideals (e.g., mission, vision, core values, and organizational purpose)
- performance standards
- purposeful actions and behaviors (e.g., expressing genuine interest, conveying authentic enthusiasm, providing pleasant surprises)
- customer expectations
- key performance indicators (KPIs)
- aspirational goals

The beauty of the Revelation Conversation is in its flexibility and uniqueness. No two conversations will sound alike. There is no rigid script that must be committed to memory and adhered to. Instead, look at the Revelation Conversation as you would any framework or guide that supports your efforts to achieve some particular result. Consider it a plan or an approach to managing performance, the absence of which would force you to wing it, unsupported and unprepared.

As a rule, I avoid scripts. I prefer natural "ways of being" to scripted "ways of doing." I realize the lead-off question in the Revelation Conversation, "Would you describe for me, from your perspective, your job role—what your job entails?" is in quotes and connotes a script. Even so, it is intended only as a guideline. To me, the language is conversational, natural, and includes every element intended in the lead-off question.

My editor suggested shortening the question to, "Would you describe, from your perspective, what your job role entails?"

Ordinarily, I jump at the chance to reduce word count. But in this case, I'm happy with the original question. You may choose my editor's shortened version. Or you may choose to revise it further. The key is not to alter it in such a way as to eliminate elements central to the question's objective. Regardless of your wording preferences, for the question to work, it must contain employees' description of their job role (this implies multiple aspects of their job role), be from their perspective (this is nonthreatening and implies there are no wrong answers),* address their job role (think about the three parts of The Anatomy of a Job Role) and what it entails (its totality; what it is composed of).

If any of these elements are missing from the question's format, you risk asking a question that is close but different, such as, "What do you do at work?"

This question sets employees up to respond in a way that deviates from the objective to reveal the totality of the employee's job role.

It's likely that employees will list their job duties and tasks in response to this question, but without a reference to the total job role, this may seem like a loaded "gotcha" question that will lead them to respond with a list of job responsibilities. You want to give employees every opportunity to reflect on the total job role before responding to the question. That way, during the conversation and when looking back on it later, they won't ascribe the job-functions-laden response to the way you phrased the question. They will instead accept that they had an incomplete understanding of their job role and that it was this perspective that shaped their response.

---

* There really are no wrong answers. Even if the employee's description is steeped in job functions, with no reference to job essence, job functions are still essential to meet or exceed customers' expectations.

The lead-off question is not designed to prove employees' ignorance about the two dimensions of every job role or its three parts. And it is not intended to provide evidence that they are disconnected from the purpose of their job roles. If anything, it will expose the supervisor or manager who poses the question as not having equipped the employee beforehand with the knowledge and awareness of their total job role.

The Revelation Conversation provides a structure to initiate individual one-on-one conversations with members of your team. The only scripted portion of that first conversation is the opening question, and even that is flexible within the guidelines as outlined above.

The rest of the conversation will flow from the employee's responses and supervisor's prompts that follow. As long as you keep the objectives of the conversation in mind, you will be successful at revealing employees' total job role, connecting their daily job responsibilities to job purpose, and inspiring greater employee engagement.

Although there may be several different revelations that occur to the employee during the Revelation Conversation, the real "aha" of the conversation is revealed when employees are challenged to confront their understanding of the totality of their job role. With few exceptions, employees will define their total job role exclusively in terms of job functions. When employees come to the realization, perhaps for the first time, that their job role consists of more than duties, tasks, responsibilities, assignments, job knowledge, job skills, transactions, protocol, policies, procedures, checklists, and reports, and that the goal of performance management does not end at competency, this opens the door to renewed awareness of possibilities and potential.

As you pursue these prospects with your staff by following up on your original conversation, you might start with, "So our single highest priority at work is to surprise and delight our customers. Think about your last shift. Can you give me an example of how you did that?"

Or you can ask for an example of something they observed a co-worker doing to reflect job purpose. Or you can solicit an aspirational example of what could be done to surprise and delight customers. You can even ask for an example of how they have been surprised and delighted as a customer themselves outside of work. Or you can share an example of something another department or location has done recently to surprise and delight customers. Or you can point to performance standards that are in place to reinforce job purpose: "The reason that we include a complimentary amuse-bouche in our table service as a standard is to exhibit our purpose to surprise and delight guests." Or you might even point to purposeful actions and behaviors such as sharing unique knowledge, for instance, about a new wine offering that will engage the customer, pique his interest, and leave a lasting positive impression.

Imagine you shared the story of a restaurant server who observed a guest examining the wine list. She then chose to share some unique knowledge to surprise and delight the guest: "There's a new red blend called 8 Years in the Desert by Dave Phinney, the winemaker behind the wildly successful red wine The Prisoner. When he sold The Prisoner in 2008, he signed a non-compete, agreeing not to make zinfandel for eight years, hence the bottle's name: 8 Years in the Desert.[1] Would you like to see if he's been able to capture lightning in a bottle a second time?"

Aside from reinforcing behaviors that support job purpose, you might just see an increase in ultra-premium wine sales!

Assuming that these types of informal one-on-one conversations about job purpose took place regularly and that the topic was also included in more formal discussions such as staff meetings, pre-shift meetings, and taste panels, how might that have impacted the dining experience of my colleague at the restaurant in Philadelphia? Would the server have offered the same tone-deaf response, aloof from mood or sensitivities, in response to his guest's desire for a Philly cheesesteak?

We already know the kitchen stocked the necessary ingredients to make the sandwich. Certainly, it wasn't unprecedented for a server to make such an accommodation. And this would be especially possible, if not likely, when job purpose is routinely discussed and reinforced in conversations between supervisors and employees. With these norms in place, it becomes unnatural for a server to display indifference toward a guest's preferences.[2]

The Revelation Conversation is not an incantation that absolves supervisors and leaders from having to do the daily work required to manage employee performance and achieve certain financial results. That said, it is the most powerful device I know of to connect employees' daily job duties to the purpose of their job role.

WHY DO WE NEED REVELATION CONVERSATIONS?

Assuming that an organization's purpose is relevant and credible (and, if not, put this book down and start there), then the Revelation Conversation is an extremely effective performance management tool to bridge the gap between that purpose and employees' daily job responsibilities (see figure 8).

Organizational or job purpose is usually shared during the onboarding process, perhaps in the new-hire orientation video or the employee handbook. Or it's posted on the corporate website or within the pages of the annual report. Or maybe it's emblazed on a button, coffee mug, or koozie you received at last year's all-employee meeting. Maybe the human resources department even provides it as a laminated wallet card. But that purpose rarely becomes a significant consideration in employees' real world of work.

The problem is that very few people, when asked, can recall their organization's mission, vision, or purpose statement without referencing their laminated wallet card.

The Revelation Conversation supports leaders and managers in their efforts to demystify job purpose and make it a meaningful part of employees' work experience. Of course, there are other vehicles for this type of work, such as the aforementioned new-hire orientation, the annual report, or the annual all-employee meeting.

Or maybe it comes up on the annual employee satisfaction survey or during performance reviews or promotional opportunities. But we already know how ineffective these strategies are as evidenced by the fact that, at most companies, very few employees can recall the organization's mission, vision, or purpose statement, much less consciously reflect it in their job performance.

If you have doubts about whether your employees will respond affirmatively to the Revelation Conversation, know that their skepticism will likely match yours. Likewise, their optimism and enthusiasm will reflect your own. In other words, the credibility of this conversation hinges on your credibility with your staff.

Give your employees the benefit of the doubt. Most employees want to do more than execute transactions and process customers until the end of another ordinary shift. They are looking for purpose in their work, to do work that is meaningful, to make a difference in the lives of their customers, and to deliver exceptional product and service quality.

KEEP THE CONVERSATION GOING

Okay, so you've initiated the Revelation Conversation with an employee. What next? You've already posed the "describe what your job role entails" question, revealed the total job role, defined job essence, articulated job purpose, and demonstrated how to connect daily job responsibilities to job purpose. Where do you go from here?

Figure 8: The Revelation Conversation Bridge

There's really no match for the effectiveness of frequent, casual one-on-one conversations. I would advise you to continue the practice and, in follow-up to that first conversation, adapt the opening question based on your recent observations and interactions with the employee.

If you work in an environment where you can observe the employee, then you will notice whether they are attempting to reflect job essence during interactions with their customers. Acknowledge their efforts in your next conversation. Does the employee have any of their own follow-up questions? Have they made any incisive comments related to job purpose during pre-shift or department meetings? Have you heard the employee make any references to job functions or job essence during interactions with other employees? These observations are all excellent starting points for ongoing conversations about job purpose.

Here are some additional prompts you might use to kick off follow-up conversations:

- Have you made any more connections between *what* you do at work and *why* you do it?
- Have you thought about anything we can do differently to support our purpose?
- Have you identified anything we're doing that contradicts our purpose?
- Have you altered the way you approach customers since our last conversation?
- What questions do you have related to our conversation about purpose at work?
- Have you done anything deliberately since our last talk to incorporate job essence into your job functions?
- Have you observed anyone reflecting job purpose in a way that made an impression on you?

An important point: I have no illusions that some of the above questions will sound unnatural to you. That's okay. You can take them as they are or make them your own. My wife dislikes using the term *job role*. She says it sounds "too HR." She prefers to say *job*. She also prefers *job responsibilities* to *job functions*, and has never loved *job essence* since it made its first appearance in my 2013 book, *Delight Your Customers*. She thinks it sounds too abstract.

If a term doesn't resonate with you, consult the definition and identify another word or phrase that captures the spirit of the term. For instance, the definition of job purpose is "the most significant element, quality, or aspect of a job role." I also refer to job purpose as "one's single highest priority at work." So there are options.

I also don't expect employees to retain terminology from your one-on-one conversations. So, when you question them about whether they have "done anything deliberately to incorporate job essence into job functions," you may very well be met with blank stares or furrowed brows. Don't be discouraged. Instead, translate these terms into language that will resonate with your audience.

The frequency with which you hold one-on-one Revelation Conversations and reinforce them through group interaction and engagement during pre-shift or staff meetings or one-on-one questioning, will increase everyone's awareness and familiarity with its tenets. Terms and concepts like job functions, job essence, and job purpose will be top of mind. The result will be a renewed enthusiasm for doing more than executing transactions and processing customers, which are the typical centerpiece of a work environment that is myopically focused on job functions.

TAKING THE REVELATION CONVERSATION ONLINE

Many of us transitioned to virtual work teams in 2020 during the COVID-19 pandemic and continue to work, collaborate, pitch, and manage performance virtually. If this describes you, you might be wondering how the Revelation Conversation works in a virtual environment.

It's true that there may be more opportunities in a face-to-face work setting to have spontaneous, informal one-on-one conversations. All that means is that you will need to be more intentional about working Revelation Conversations into your virtual one-on-ones with employees.

Collaboration tools like Slack, Zoom, Microsoft Teams, Google Docs, Facebook's Workplace, and others enable teams to work together regardless of whether they are on-site, entirely virtual, or somewhere in between. For those of you who have been holding many virtual conversations that used to be face-to-face, such as job interviews, coaching calls, and performance appraisals, the Revelation Conversation will seem like a natural extension of those discussions.

The beauty of the Revelation Conversation is that, unlike a job interview, coaching call, or performance appraisal, it is intended to be informal. It doesn't require a meeting invitation for the recipient to attend "Revelation Conversation at 10 a.m. ET." Because it is informal, it can simply be folded into an existing one-on-one call. After the first minute or two of checking in with each other, you might simply say, "Before we get started, I've got a question for you. From your perspective, how would you describe your job role—what your job entails?"

And, with that, you're into the Revelation Conversation.

I recently attended a webinar led by Aaron Hurst of Imperative, a peer coaching platform used to conduct more than thirty thousand virtual conversations between December 2020 and early September 2021. A third of call participants, prior to the virtual coaching calls, felt as though they were not growing personally but were hungry for opportunities to invest in their professional growth and fulfillment. By analyzing outcomes from the coaching calls, Imperative isolated benefits in three areas: relationships, impact, and growth. Specifically, 89 percent of call participants shared that connections made through these virtual conversations created meaningful and sustained relationships. Fifty-two percent of participants claimed to have taken actions after the conversation that increased their impact. And 57 percent reported they took actions that helped them to grow.[3]

It's clear that whether these discussions are online, over the phone, or face-to-face, employees thirst for one-on-one conversations that center on relationships, impact, and growth.

YES, IT HAS TO BE ONE-ON-ONE

Resist the urge to be expedient and hold the conversation with your entire team. You will dilute the impact of the conversation and sacrifice many of its benefits. Perhaps the biggest loss will be to forfeit the one-on-one time you have with each member of your team to discuss their job role, job purpose, and how they describe the connection between their daily job duties and the purpose of their job role.

A *Harvard Business Review* study found the most basic form of communication, one-on-ones, can have a massive impact on the staff's opinion of leadership and the degree of employee engagement: "When a manager doesn't meet with employees one-on-one at all . . . employees are four times as likely to be disengaged . . . and are twice as likely to view leadership more unfavorably compared to those who meet with their managers regularly." In the companies analyzed, the average manager spent thirty minutes every three weeks with each of their employees. Perhaps unsurprisingly, employees who got little to no one-on-one time with their managers were more likely to be disengaged. On the flip side, those who got twice the number of one-on-ones with their manager relative to their peers were 67 percent less likely to be disengaged.[4]

"There is no other way to create a relationship with a [team member] than to sit down [one-on-one] and spend time with them," advises Mark Horstman, cohost of the popular weekly *Manager Tools* podcast. Since its 2005 launch, the program has received millions of downloads and topped the business category of the People's Choice Podcast Awards several times.

"We know everybody's busy, and we wish there was a better way," adds Mr. Horstman. "We wish we could give you a pill, we could snap our fingers, we could hypnotize you, we could wave a wand, whatever. We wish we could do that."[5] But there is no substitute for setting aside time to connect with your employees one-on-one. And there is no other way for leaders to initiate the Revelation Conversation. Shocking, right? Don't pass up the opportunity to hold this one-on-one conversation with each member of your team. You have everything to gain and nothing to lose by trying.

Exercise

Schedule your first Revelation Conversation with a specific employee with the goal of initiating the conversation with each member of your staff in the coming days or weeks.

Below, write the name (or initials) of the employee, place, date, and time you will hold the conversation.

Name: _____ Date: _____

Place: _____ Time: _____

Using the framework below, prepare for the conversation, paying particular attention to being

- prepared to accept personal responsibility for the employee's probable incomplete view of their job role
- grounded in the organization's purpose, culture, corporate ideals, and performance standards, and how these connect to the employee's job purpose
- ready with examples of purposeful job-specific actions and behaviors (e.g., being observant, taking initiative, displaying a sense of urgency, sharing unique knowledge, using appropriate humor)

Lead-off question. Begin the conversation by asking the employee this question:

1. *"Would you describe for me, from your perspective, your job role—what your job entails?"*

They will likely provide a list dominated by job functions.

Validate the response, accept personal responsibility for omissions, and reveal the totality of the job role. It is critical that you do not appear to judge their response and, assuming it is devoid of any reference to purposeful actions or behaviors, imply that the employee should be aware of a dimension of their job role that was omitted. Instead, validate the job functions listed (they're essential) and accept responsibility for the employee's incomplete view of their job role that led to the omission of actions or behaviors that reflect job purpose. You might say:

2. *"That's an impressive list of job functions, the duties and tasks related to your job role. All of those things are important and necessary—even critical to our success. Though, if that's how you would describe the totality of your job role, then I have explained your job to you incompletely. Job functions make up only one aspect of your job role. The other dimension of your job role is job essence."*

They will likely ask, "What is job essence?"

Clarify job essence. Then you will clarify by saying:

3. *"Job essence is how you reflect, through actions and behaviors, the purpose of your job role; your single highest priority at work."*

They will likely ask, "What's that?"

Clarify job purpose. And then you will say:

4. *"Your single highest priority at work is to* _____
   _____*."* (This
   may match the job purpose that you articulated for
   your own job role in chapter 3.)

Then they might ask, "How do I do that?"

The payoff. As mentioned, the conversation that follows, besides
serving customers directly, might just be the best use of your time at
work. This is a great opportunity to

- reinforce performance standards
- inspire the employee to realize their potential at work
- raise expectations and challenge the employee
  professionally
- demonstrate support for the employee's success in
  their job role
- reflect openness and honesty in communication
- show personal interest in the employee
- build the relationship
- convey that you are a purpose-driven leader

5 | Aligning Actions and Behaviors with Purpose

In 2016, I came across a story in the *New York Times*, "The Secret Lives of Hotel Doormen." The article featured Gary Sykes, a remarkable doorman at the Thompson Chicago, a boutique hotel located in the Gold Coast district, which is just north of the downtown Loop. His customer service quality, as detailed in the article, was so impressive that I was moved to search for the hotel's address and put a note in the mail to commend him.

What stood out to me was that, in a fast-paced environment that is susceptible to being highly transactional, Mr. Sykes was deliberate about controlling the speed and quality of his interactions with guests. For example, it's expected of a hotel doorman to open the car door for a guest arriving by taxi and retrieve their suitcase from the trunk—perhaps glancing at the luggage tag to obtain the guest's name in the process. Contrast this performance with the care and attentiveness displayed by Mr. Sykes, who habitually inspects arriving vehicles for stray cellphones, wallets, and sunglasses that may have been inadvertently left behind. He also verifies guests' names by cross-referencing the name on the luggage tag with the up-to-date, airline-issued baggage label to avoid mistakes.[1]

Rather than imposing his services on guests in a way that could be seen as smarmy or a play for tips, Mr. Sykes makes himself available to guests by detecting cues that would indicate their level of need and receptivity to his services. "In effect, Mr. Sykes's method is to develop a profile of each person he encounters—which he is constantly updating—and calibrating accordingly. To the pair of middle-aged women on their way to Gibson's Steakhouse, he was the vicarious wingman. 'Have the Turtle Pie with ice cream,' he counseled. 'It is very fattening but delicious.'"

To the overnight business travelers intent on handling their own luggage—the "one-baggers" in doorman parlance—he is the discreet aide-de-camp, opening doors and tending to cars without belaboring the interaction. 'Let's get you inside,' he will say. 'My brain is yours. Take what you need and leave me the rest.'"[2]

What separates noteworthy customer service quality from its unremarkable counterpart, regardless of the prevailing corporate culture, often comes down to the one-on-one interactions customers have with service providers. If they happen to get Gary Sykes as their doorman during a trip to Chicago, then they will likely have a memorable guest experience. But if they happen to get a doorman who lacks Mr. Sykes's initiative, perceptiveness, and demeanor, the quality of their experience is left to chance.

In his own words, "You can put anyone here you want, but you can't put a Gary here." He's correct—and he makes my point. Thanks, Gary.

Too often, the quality of a customer's experience is *reliant on the employee involved*, the employee they happen to get. The goal of customer service training should be to provide a consistent level of customer service *regardless of the employee involved*. Although *behaviors* such as taking initiative, perceptiveness, and one's demeanor are beyond the reach of most training program objectives (but within the scope of predicative selection software), employers can train staff to perform *actions* such as checking the back seat of cabs for stray items or cross-referencing the name on the luggage tag with the airline-issued baggage label.

This chapter presents readers with ways to reflect job purpose in both mandated and rehearsed *actions* and discretionary, often spontaneous, *behaviors* that are emblematic of purpose-driven, engaged employees. I will reveal what I have found to be the key to providing consistent, highly engaged employee performance, over time, by design, rather than inconsistently, here and there, by chance: *incorporate job essence* (inspecting the back seat of cabs, verifying the guest's name) *into job functions* (welcoming hotel guests). I will also discuss the importance of seeking frontline employee input to identify purposeful actions and behaviors that can be operationalized to replicate exceptional customer service quality.

The focus of this chapter is to align employee actions and behaviors with purpose. And since the recommended way to increase the consistency with which these actions and behaviors are displayed by employees is to incorporate job essence into job functions, now is a good time to review the following terms so there's no confusion.

ACTION: The process of doing something, typically to achieve an aim.

BEHAVIOR: The way in which a person conducts oneself, especially toward others.

JOB FUNCTIONS: Any of a group of related actions (duties and tasks) performed by an employee in a particular job role.

JOB ESSENCE: The reflection, through actions and behaviors, of job purpose as evidenced by the employee's unique role-based contributions in support of organizational purpose.

It is important to distinguish between mandatory actions, required of employees as part of standard processes, and voluntary behaviors that, by definition, cannot be mandated; only suggested, encouraged, and modeled.

JOB FUNCTIONS VERSUS JOB ESSENCE

When you begin to reflexively think of a job role in terms of its three parts (job knowledge, job skills, and job purpose) and two dimensions (job functions and job essence), you will become attuned to the absence or presence of job essence during the interactions you have with service providers, as in these examples:

BARTENDER A TO A CUSTOMER, WHEN ASKED HOW A MINT JULEP IS MADE: "A mint julep is made with simple syrup or sugar, bourbon whiskey, and muddled mint sprigs."

BARTENDER B TO THE SAME CUSTOMER AFTER DETAILING THE DRINK'S INGREDIENTS: "Did you know that the official mint julep of the Kentucky Derby is not made with bourbon? It's made with Early Times whiskey. Because Early Times is aged in second-hand barrels passed down from the Old Forrester bourbon distillery—and since bourbon distillers can only use their barrels once—it's not actually bourbon."

Bartender A clearly has job knowledge—he knows the ingredients required to make a mint julep. And the adeptness with which he can consistently mix a mint julep cocktail will demonstrate his technical job skills. It is likely that bartender A is competent at executing his job functions.

Bartender B's choice to share unique knowledge with the customer provides insight into his personality, attitude toward his job, and engagement level. The gesture also expresses genuine interest in the customer rather than simply processing his request as just another drink order. In doing so, he is reflecting job essence.

SERVER A TO A RESTAURANT GUEST: "Beet carpaccio. Got it. Will that be all?"

SERVER B TO THE SAME RESTAURANT GUEST: "Beet carpaccio is an excellent choice! I've had a chance to sample it. The subtle flavors of thinly shaved beets marinated in citrus juice and spices burst into an array of tastes."

Rather than simply executing a diner's order like server A, server B offers a sincere and specific compliment, shares unique knowledge, and conveys authentic enthusiasm for the guest's selection.

Taking diners' orders is a mandatory job function. Offering a compliment, sharing unique "insider" knowledge, and conveying enthusiasm are elective. While you can count on your order being taken (eventually) as a function of the server's job role, you cannot count on her to be interested and engaged. Displaying job essence is voluntary and reflects the higher purpose of the job role.

HOTEL CONCIERGE A TO A GUEST: "That restaurant is located in the Gaslamp Quarter."

HOTEL CONCIERGE B TO THE SAME GUEST: "That restaurant is in the Gaslamp Quarter. That part of downtown is named after the gas lamps that lined the streets in the early 1900s when the area was a red-light district known as the Stingaree. The name was probably derived from the fierce stingrays in the San Diego Bay. It was said that you could be stung as badly in the Stingaree as in the bay!"

Hotel concierge A demonstrates that he is familiar with the location of restaurants in downtown San Diego, a job function of a hotel concierge in that locale. Hotel concierge B chooses to share unique knowledge about the region and convey authentic enthusiasm for the area's history.

SERVER A TO GUEST: "Tonight, our featured appetizer is the Foie Gras Torchon. Can I start you out with one?"

SERVER B TO THE SAME GUEST: "Our chef trained at the prestigious Auguste Escoffier School in Boulder, Colorado, and apprenticed at Le Bernardin in New York City. She also traveled to France to refine her knowledge of French delicacies like truffles, escargot, and foie gras. In fact, our Foie Gras Torchon is our featured appetizer. May I tempt you with an order?"

Server A demonstrates her job knowledge, specifically, the name of tonight's featured appetizer. Server B elevates the interaction by reflecting job essence—sharing unique knowledge about the chef's background. Seriously, after learning about the chef's deep knowledge of French cuisine, why wouldn't you want to sample the featured appetizer?

In each of the above examples, service providers who exude job essence while executing their job functions give their customers insight into their interest and engagement levels. And since each of these job roles is partially compensated through gratuities, you can imagine that gross tips are higher for those who choose to acquire and share unique knowledge, offer sincere and specific compliments, convey authentic enthusiasm, or in other ways reflect job essence.

Importantly, it's not zero-sum: execute job functions or reflect job essence. You need to do both if your goal is to make a lasting positive impression. It's interesting to learn about the history of the official mint julep of the Kentucky Derby, but not at the expense of a well-made cocktail. And I will appreciate the chef's background even more if the server delivers the featured appetizer on time and at the proper temperature.

In each of the above examples, the behaviors modeled reflect the personality and unique flair of the service provider. It's unnatural to mandate behaviors like expressing *genuine* interest, offering *sincere* and specific compliments, and conveying *authentic* enthusiasm. But that doesn't mean you can't suggest, encourage, and model these behaviors for your staff. Over time, they will be made aware of your expectations, be encouraged by your affirmation, and glean insights from your example. And soon they will find their own unique voice, style, and individual flair.

INCORPORATING JOB ESSENCE INTO JOB FUNCTIONS

To make job purpose come alive, to make it real and actionable as job essence, requires that you have a deep reserve of stories, illustrations, and anecdotes of purposeful actions and behaviors that you have performed personally, seen others perform, or have considered as possibilities. To be a purpose-driven leader, you must be prepared with examples of how to link job duties and tasks to job purpose.

Do you recall the example used by the restaurant manager in chapter 4—the story behind the wine 8 Years in the Desert? That illustration depicted the relationship between sharing unique knowledge, creating a captivating experience for the guest, and selling a bottle of ultra-premium wine. Because the server was first *interested* in learning more about the wines offered, she was *interesting*, refreshing, and memorable.

Sometimes the difference between mediocrity and excellence is subtle—literally, the word(s) chosen. Consider these examples:

Given Disney's moniker, The Happiest Place on Earth, you would not expect a cast member working at the stroller rental kiosk to say, "Keep your receipt separate from your stroller to obtain a replacement in case someone *steals* it." Theft? At the happiest place on earth? If this were to be the case, instead of thinking about which section of the park to visit first, guests might question the security of their stroller and other belongings.

Because Disney cast members are trained extensively to display actions and behaviors that are aligned with its purpose, one would instead expect for the stroller attendant to phrase the message this way: "Please keep your receipt separate from your stroller to obtain a replacement in case someone *leaves with yours by mistake*."

Now, I know that theft happens—even at The Happiest Place on Earth—but to preserve the magic and reflect job purpose, cast members should not broadcast it.

Here's another illustration that shows the importance of word choice. When my children were young, we visited Rainforest Cafe while on vacation in Anaheim, California. The restaurant's concept, a tropical rainforest theme, is described on its website: "Part adventure, part restaurant and wholly entertaining for the entire family, the Rainforest Cafe re-creates a tropical rainforest with waterfalls, lush vegetation, and indigenous creatures."

After being seated, our waiter approached the table and provided a brief introduction to the restaurant that concluded with, "The gorilla *goes off* every fifteen minutes."

Incidentally, I learned on the company's website that the gorilla's name was Bamba. I couldn't help but think how our experience would have been better, and more consistent with the promise touted on the website, if the server had said, "Bamba, the gorilla, *wakes up* every fifteen minutes."

Now, I realize that the gorilla is an animatronic puppet and doesn't really wake up, but Rainforest Cafe employees should maintain the magic—especially for young explorers.

How much of a difference does word choice make? At most fast-food restaurants, you're likely to hear "No problem" in response to a guest who thanks an employee.

Saying "No problem" isn't the end of the world. But the idea is to embrace a higher personal standard of customer service quality that recognizes a distinction in the way you communicate with your friends outside of work and the way you speak to customers at work.

As Dee Ann Turner, a former Chick-fil-A executive and the author of *It's My Pleasure*, shared, "When a guest says thank you, what you hear back from our employees is, 'my pleasure' because what it really means is, 'it's my pleasure to serve our customers.'"[3]

I assure you that once you alter your perspective and commit to a new level of performance, former behaviors that, even unwittingly, reflect indifference will now be glaring assaults on your enhanced performance standards.

Even simple words such as *please* and *thank you* that connote respect and appreciation toward customers can have an impact. In *QSR Magazine*'s annual drive-thru report, employees at Chick-fil-A were the most likely of the fifteen chains evaluated to say "please" and "thank you," and to smile at customers. According to the report, Chick-fil-A employees said "thank you" in 95.2 percent of drive-thru encounters, based on data from nearly two thousand visits to fifteen restaurant chains. For comparison, KFC had a "thank you" rate of 84.9 percent. McDonald's rate was 78.4 percent, putting it in fourteenth place out of the fifteen chains analyzed.[4]

Does Chick-fil-A's focus on pleasantries matter? Sales increased by 17 percent in 2019, generating more than $10.5 billion and propelling it past Burger King, Wendy's, Taco Bell, and Subway. Now the third-largest restaurant chain in the United States behind Starbucks and McDonald's, Chick-fil-A shows no signs of letting up. Despite being closed on Sundays, Chick-fil-A stores average $4.58 million per store in annual sales, more than any other fast-food restaurant chain.[5]

Besides language, here are some other ways that Chick-fil-A incorporates essence into function in a manner that ignites engagement and makes a difference to customers. Employees often walk through the drive-thru line taking orders via tablets so that customers do not have to wait as long.[6] They are also known for going above and beyond by, for instance, escorting in-store customers to and from their cars under an umbrella when it rains. The result? In the latest American Customer Satisfaction Index (ACSI) Restaurant Study for 2020–21, customer satisfaction with the limited-service (fast-food) restaurant industry is 78 on the ACSI's zero-to-100 scale. Chick-fil-A topped the industry for the seventh consecutive year with an ACSI score of 83.[7]

OPERATIONALIZING JOB ESSENCE

Have you ever been a passenger on the Jungle Cruise ride at Disneyland? The cast member acting as the skipper on your cruise has been carefully screened via Disney's sophisticated selection process, so you already expect that they will be exceptional. You will not be surprised to be greeted by an engaged, smiling, uniformed tour guide who conveys authentic enthusiasm for hosting guests on the cruise. While the uniform can be mandated, each of the behaviors listed is voluntary. The cast member chooses to display them.

As the ride gets underway, the guide transitions from spontaneous banter (behavior) with guests to a carefully rehearsed script (an action) that incorporates job essence into the job functions associated with acting as the skipper of the Jungle Cruise. This job essence may take the form of sharing unique knowledge, using appropriate humor, or providing pleasant surprises.

As you approach a large open stretch of water, your guide might say, "We're going down the Nile River. At 4,132 miles, it's the longest river in the world. It goes on for Niles and Niles and Niles. . . . If you don't believe me, then you're in denial."

Then, as you encounter a hostile (animatronic) rhino on the right side of the boat, your guide says, "That's why you don't want to argue with a rhino. They always get their point across."

By carefully crafting their tour scripts, within the parameters established by Disney management and in alignment with Disney's

purpose ("We create happiness by providing the finest in entertainment for people of all ages, everywhere"), cast members are
intentional about incorporating job essence *into* their job functions.
Whether or not you laugh, learn something new, or are pleasantly
surprised on the Jungle Cruise ride should not hinge on the skipper you happen to get. Embedding unique knowledge, appropriate
humor, and pleasant surprises into the script ensures a consistent
experience from cruise to cruise *regardless of the cast member involved.*

Codifying the "voluntary" behaviors of sharing unique knowledge, using appropriate humor, and providing a pleasant surprise
into the script (job function) used by the skipper to guide a boatload
of passengers along the Jungle Cruise is an illustration of operationalizing job essence. Of course, once a behavior becomes operationalized, it's no longer voluntary and left to chance. It has become
systematized and ingrained in the process. As it pertains to the Jungle Cruise, it ensures consistency from one skipper, cruise, and customer experience to the next.

I have been asked, "If it's so easy to do, why not add job essence
to every process and eliminate poor customer service entirely?"

Aside from the obvious issues of inevitable breakdowns in the
process, whether related to personnel, maintenance, technology, or
some other factor, there will always be variables that are beyond
your control, such as weather, customer expectations, emergencies,
and the like. And then there is the human element that is difficult to
predict, varying from one person to another and from one day to the
next. The idea is to control what you can control. Operationalizing
job essence is within your control; however, the attitudes, positiv-
ity, and engagement levels of employees are outside of your control
(not your influence; your control).

To illustrate, consider the professional waiters at Sparks Steak
House in New York City. On any given night, you can witness them
deftly changing linen tablecloths between dinner and dessert courses
without exposing the wooden tabletop underneath. Throughout the

exhibition, plates, silverware, and, importantly, barware *never leave the table*. It's really quite genius—and is an example of operational-izing job essence (a mesmerizing performance) by embedding it into a job function (clearing the table, changing the tablecloth between courses). It is a mandatory choreographed action that has been re-hearsed, perfected, and inserted into a standard process.

It's true that this elegant routine (an action) can be performed by a surly waiter (behavior) who's ready to get the hell out of there. Again, behaviors (smiling, making eye contact, being interested, car-ing) are voluntary and cannot be mandated.

CONNECT TO PURPOSE

A senior executive, interviewed for an article that appeared in the *Wall Street Journal*, advised that leaders must create "an environ-ment where you can have a higher purpose," acknowledging, "It puts more pressure on managers and leaders in large companies to be really connected with their [purpose at work] to ensure that employ-ees are getting that."[8]

This sentiment reinforces the point that purpose statements can-not simply reside on a website or a laminated card that tucks neatly inside one's wallet. Employees' higher purpose must be brought to life as job essence and made real in the daily actions and behaviors of employees at all levels of the organization.

As noted in chapter 3, an auto parts retailer revealed to its store employees that they have a higher purpose beyond simply stocking shelves, ringing up merchandise, and processing returns. Company leadership wanted to transform employees' perception of their job role from retail clerks to consultative advisers.

The company screens applicants during the hiring process to val-idate their knowledge of automobiles, so it's no surprise that most of the retail store employees are "car people." In addition, employees receive regular product training from the company and its manu-factures' representatives. On top of that, the company developed a web-based training program that reinforced how employees were uniquely qualified to provide a "peek behind the curtain," to educate customers and, possibly, demystify the somewhat intimidating world of auto parts and repairs. And so, the job purpose of store employees, their single highest priority at work, became *to build relationships with customers by solving their problems.*

This retailer embedded the actions and mindset indicative of an expert adviser whose priority is the long-term best interest of the customer and vehicle, into employees' job functions (obtaining product specifications, answering basic questions, ringing up merchandise, obtaining a valid method of payment, issuing a receipt, etc.). Here is an example from the web-based training program of how the store employees were instructed to manifest job essence during actual customer encounters inside the store:

A customer asks about motor oil. Which answers below give you the best chance of being seen as a consultative adviser whose single highest priority at work is to build relationships by solving problems, rather than as a retail clerk? Select all that apply.

A. Verify the correct oil viscosity, locate the bottles, and sell the customer five quarts of motor oil.
B. Suggest other items the customer might need for the job, such as oil filter, oil filter removal wrench, funnel, drain pan, etc.
C. Remark that it can be a messy job and to consider adding a pair of gloves and oil absorber pads.
D. Include a list of local motor oil recycling locations for the customer to safely dispose of the used motor oil.

The best answers that reflect job essence are B, C, and D. By expressing genuine interest in the customer's need and taking the initiative to share unique (and, perhaps, even unexpected) knowledge, each of these responses position the employee as a trusted adviser who has the long-term best interest of the customer and vehicle in mind, rather than a retail clerk who merely executes transactions.

Now, some might refer to responses B and C as being upselling or cross-selling tactics designed to increase store sales and profits at the expense of customer satisfaction. Interestingly, a 2021 study by Customer Care Measurement and Consulting (CCMC) detailed the benefits of cross-selling to customers. Cross-selling was rated as the number one delighter for increased willingness to spend. Seventy-seven percent of the respondents who were delighted through their cross-selling experience reported that they will talk positively about the brand. According to CCMC Vice Chairman John Goodman, "For each customer delighted by cross-selling, it's reasonable to assume that it will result in three new customers via word of mouth."[9]

Remember that the employee's priority is to build relationships by solving problems. If a store clerk can, by anticipating the customer's needs (or future problems, as it were), save them a frustrating return trip to the store to purchase an oil filter, drain pan, or another item they didn't know they needed until they needed it, then they are going to remember and appreciate that as exceptional customer service. This gesture has also reduced the effort needed to accomplish the customer's objective to change their car's oil. Depending on how tightly the oil filter was screwed in, they might really appreciate having an oil filter removal wrench. The clerk has solved that problem while simultaneously increasing store sales and profits. This isn't traditional upselling where customer loyalty is subordinated to bad profits; it's mutually beneficial anticipatory service.

HOW DO YOU MANAGE JOB ESSENCE?

I've often repeated the truth that exceptional customer service is always voluntary. When pundits challenge that notion, suggesting that employers can mandate exceptional customer service quality, my usual response is that while employers can enforce dress codes, they can't force employees to express genuine interest, offer sincere compliments, or convey authentic enthusiasm. These behaviors are voluntary. Employees choose to demonstrate them—or, more likely, choose not to. Besides, forced interest, compliments, and enthusiasm are uncomfortable for everyone involved.

Part of this debate is semantics. Are exceptional customer service behaviors *optional*? Of course not. But they are voluntary. You cannot force an employee to deliver exceptional customer service any more than you can make a customer be loyal.

I don't know whether Gary Sykes, the hotel doorman we met at the beginning of the chapter, is aware of his job purpose. I don't know that his supervisor has ever held the Revelation Conversation with him or that he knows what job essence is. The fact is, there will always be a handful of superstar employees that are highly engaged and reflect job essence whether or not they know what it is. This explains why the experience you have at select restaurants may hinge on the server's section in which you happen to be seated. But happenstance is not a recipe for consistency, whether in customer service quality or employee engagement levels.

Whenever I am asked how to hold employees accountable for displaying job essence, which is largely volitional, I respond that it's similar to how you hold employees accountable for executing mandatory job functions. For actions, it's simple.

Actions—even those that reflect job essence—are concrete and quantifiable (e.g., providing a thirteenth bagel to surprise and delight a customer with a baker's dozen, gift wrapping a purchase, or sending a thank-you note to a client). Therefore, actions that reflect job essence can be mandated. You can easily require that an employee add a thirteenth bagel to an order or slip booties over his work shoes before entering a client's home. You can incorporate those actions into job descriptions, processes, standards, policies, and procedures. Then, you can use those standards to manage performance. If employees choose not to reflect job essence when it's a part of the performance standard, then they will be subject to performance management measures—just like employees who fail to properly execute required job functions.

Managing behaviors differs from managing actions. Behavior is more subjective; it cannot be mandated in the same way as actions. By their nature, expressing genuine interest by smiling, making eye contact, and establishing rapport are voluntary. So is offering a sincere and specific compliment. And so is conveying authentic enthusiasm. It is simply not possible to coerce an employee to be interested, enthusiastic, or engaged. It's not natural.

So, what are you to do? How is it possible to enforce behaviors that are voluntary? I have three suggestions and they are all linked to observation and feedback. In the absence of monitoring and tallying the frequency of smiles, eye contact, and other voluntary behaviors (don't do this; it's awkward), you must instead model purposeful behavior yourself, publicly recognize when others exhibit desired behaviors, and keep the conversation going about what purposeful behaviors look like.

Model purposeful behaviors. The late restaurateur and speaker Bob Farrell championed the phrase "What they see is what you'll get."[10] If employees see you exhibiting purposeful behaviors, then they will be more likely to do the same. Too often, leadership trumpets service and engagement levels that they themselves do not consistently model. It's no wonder so many improvement campaigns lack credibility with employees and ultimately fail. An example I often point out in my consulting work is the discrepancy between the quality and cleanliness of areas intended for employees and areas reserved for customers. Most employee locker rooms are dingier than facilities accessible to customers. And break rooms and cafeterias—places where employees go to reenergize for the remainder of their shift—are often sterile, nondescript, and uninspiring. If you hope to inspire employees to provide exceptional product and service quality to customers, you must first provide exceptional product and service quality to them.

Recognize when others exhibit purposeful behaviors. I recall a Gallup study that revealed that 65 percent of US workers claimed to have received no performance-based feedback from their immediate supervisor during the previous twelve months.[11] And for those that do receive regular feedback, the majority pertains to job functions and management controls such as systems, standards, and measurements. Make it a point to notice, recognize, and share instances of employees displaying purposeful actions and behaviors. Pre-shift meetings and team huddles are an easy, informal way to highlight these contributions. Point out examples that you witnessed personally and invite others to share their own observations.

Keep the conversation going. There are many actions, beyond offering helpful tips and suggestions, that you can take to prompt desired performance from your employees. A colleague of mine poses the question, "What did you see me do?" to subordinates. The goal is to develop their job knowledge, job skills, and ability to reflect job purpose. He told me that in addition to employees relating back to him what they had observed, thus reinforcing their learning and increasing their competency, this question has the added benefit of heightening their awareness and attention to detail. They know that at any time he might ask them, "What did you see me do?"

As Yankees legend Yogi Berra noted, "You can observe a lot just by watching." By incorporating job essence into job functions in the form of purposeful actions and behaviors, you will transform purpose from an abstract statement on the company website to a tangible part of employees' real world of work. Not only can this lead to greater engagement, these actions and behaviors can be used to create movement and signal progress toward the work group's key performance indicators, as I'll discuss in the next chapter.

Exercise

Reflect on the examples in this chapter of employees that are engaged in more than simply executing job tasks. Now, what are some ways that you can incorporate job essence into job functions to elevate the quality of the interactions or deliverables for which you are responsible?

Here's an example from my own world of work to get you started:

Each year around the holidays, I receive a flurry of well-intentioned electronic greeting cards to ring in the season. These are generally emailed en masse to a large distribution list. I do not look forward to receiving these. Nor do I archive the links with the intention of opening them between sips of eggnog as I sit in my easy chair next to the fireplace while Ella Fitzgerald sings holiday classics in the background. In truth, I don't open all of them.

When I started my own business in 2007, I elected to send annual holiday cards to clients, prospects, and colleagues to spread holiday cheer and look ahead with optimism to the approaching year. I hire an illustrator to create an image that I've had in mind that becomes the front cover of the card.

On the interior of the card, together with a holiday greeting, I include a line or two pertaining to the cover illustration. The cards are printed on quality paper stock. I sign each card, often including a note that relates to a personal or professional experience that we shared earlier in the year. The cards are placed in a linen envelope, a holiday stamp is affixed, and the cards are mailed. This extra effort results in dozens of conversations in the months of December and January that, I suspect, would not have occurred if I chose to blast a link to my distribution list.

In this example, I choose to incorporate job essence (attention to detail and personalized care) into a job function (the process of sending holiday greetings) to elevate the experience from ordinary to extraordinary. This is the purpose of my job role, my single highest priority at work.

Now, it's your turn. Think about your own job role. What are three ways that you can incorporate job essence (purposeful actions and behaviors) into job functions (duties, tasks, processes) to elevate the quality of your interactions or deliverables?

1. _____

   _____

   _____

2. _____

   _____

   _____

3. _____

   _____

   _____

PART III

INSPIRING GREATER EMPLOYEE ENGAGEMENT

6 | Tracking Purposeful Actions and Behaviors

Corporations measure everything from customer satisfaction to market share. These variables produce metrics that executives use to monitor progress toward the organization's goals. But few organizations with customer-facing employees bother, for example, to quantify the frequency with which their employees introduce themselves to customers. Why does such a seemingly trivial detail matter? A multinational retailer client of mine conducted a customer satisfaction survey analysis that revealed some interesting findings that explain why.

When customers can recall an employee by name, their overall satisfaction is 20 percent higher and their likelihood to return (a key indicator of customer loyalty) is 11 percent higher. If this is true, then the corollary is also true: when employees introduce themselves to customers, key performance indicators (KPIs) such as overall satisfaction, repurchase rates, the likelihood to recommend the company, and the probability of spending more will increase. Without a connection, loyalty seldom occurs. And customers do not connect with a nameless person. Imagine the impact that employees can have on these KPIs by increasing the percentage of proactive introductions on the sales floor.

Part III, "Inspiring Greater Employee Engagement," consists of chapters 6 and 7. The objective of chapter 6 is for the reader to be able to establish a scoring mechanism to record, post, tabulate, compare, and correlate leading indicators with lagging indicators. In this chapter I will present a method you can use to involve team members in executing, tracking, and measuring purposeful actions and behaviors that have the ability to influence KPIs and create progress toward the organization's North Star and the team's aspirational goal. The objective of chapter 7, "Creating Team Alignment," is for the reader to be able to craft a team rallying cry using a set of proven criteria. This oft-overlooked device enables you to inspire team members in the collective pursuit of a common aspirational goal.

An action or behavior that incorporates job essence into a job function, such as introducing yourself to a customer, can be a leading indicator for a team or organizational KPI. *Leading indicators* are actions that suggest future success, while *lagging indicators* like KPIs reflect the results of past performance. Wearing a seat belt is a leading indicator of automobile safety that correlates with the lagging indicators of serious injury or death in the event of a car crash. On a construction site, wearing a hard hat is a leading indicator of safety that correlates with the lagging indicator of workplace accidents. In a sales environment, prospecting activity is a leading indicator of sales success that correlates with the lagging indicator of scheduled product demonstrations. And the frequency of product demos, in turn, is a leading indicator of sales success that correlates with the lagging indicators of signed contracts and new business revenue.

When you and your team are faced with a specific target to hit over the next month, quarter, or year, it can be intimidating. Your first question might be, "Where do we start?" Leading indicators are a great tool to employ for a daunting challenge like achieving a certain lagging indicator (e.g., overall satisfaction score, net promoter score, or customer effort score). This is where the fun begins. In addition to helping you and your team reach your quotas, goals, and KPI targets, incorporating job essence into job functions (and tracking the frequency of execution) will keep your team engaged and motivated in its pursuit of the aspirational goal.

To revisit the multinational retailer's customer satisfaction survey analysis from the front of the chapter, the data further revealed that when customers encounter an employee on the sales floor, they have an overall better experience, as evidenced by 18 percent increases reported in both overall satisfaction and likelihood to recommend.

In addition to double-digit increases in overall satisfaction and likelihood to recommend (another key indicator of customer loyalty), customers who encountered an employee on the sales floor spent an average of 28 percent more. And if they were highly satisfied with the employee's friendliness, then average spending increased another 3 percentage points, to 31 percent more.

Although a 31 percent increase in customer spending is substantial, the data also revealed that nearly half of all customers (47 percent) don't encounter an employee on the sales floor. And this raises the question: If we know that customers who report encountering an employee on the sales floor are more satisfied overall, are more likely to recommend your store or brand to others, and spend an average of 28 to 31 percent more, why doesn't *every* customer encounter an employee on the sales floor?

Here's how my client used purposeful actions and behaviors as leading indicators to positively impact lagging indicators (overall satisfaction, intent to recommend, and average spend). I advised my client to assemble her team, share these survey findings, and then brainstorm ways they could be deliberate about initiating customer encounters without being intrusive or appearing to hover. Here's what they came up with:

1. Initiate contact rather than waiting for customers to seek assistance.
2. Practice the 15 × 5 rule: Within 15 feet, make eye contact, smile, and nod (while looking for cues from the

customer that they may require assistance). Within 5 feet, make eye contact, smile, and offer an appropriate greeting and provide assistance (e.g., "Good morning! Is there something I can help you find?").

3. Be intentional about wearing a name tag, positioning it so that it is visible to customers, and offering your name during interactions with customers, whether face-to-face or over the phone.

4. Ask customers who have selected a clothing item if they would like a dressing room to try it on.

5. Offer to retrieve a shopping cart or basket for a customer holding several items.

6. Anticipate needs by scanning for and approaching customers who appear to be lost or looking for something.

7. Invite customers to join the store's loyalty program.

8. Provide an application for the store's rewards credit card.

By encouraging employees to initiate such encounters, these opportunities are not left to chance. Instead, these "chance" encounters occur by design. And when they do, survey analysis suggests they will make customers 18 percent more likely to recommend the store to others while spending 28 to 31 percent more, on average.

TRACKING LEADING AND LAGGING INDICATORS

What normally happens is that a supervisor gleans insights about purposeful actions and behaviors from personal observations, interactions with customers, or conversations with employees. With the best of intentions, they share this information with employees during pre-shift or department meetings with the goal of heightening everyone's awareness and improving results. But if that's where the discussion ends, it is likely to have minimal impact over the long term, and even if KPIs (lagging indicators) improve, it will be difficult to ascribe these improvements to any one contributing leading indicator.

That's why it is critical to track and measure how these purposeful actions and behaviors influence the KPIs that matter most. And not only to track and measure their impact, but to make the numbers highly visible so employees can see and interact with them daily. Years ago, I met a senior executive who worked in global safety and security who was fond of saying, "Memories fade. Ink doesn't. Write it down." I agree. I recommend keeping a large whiteboard in a visible place that everyone must walk by. But whether you use a physical whiteboard in a face-to-face environment, a digital scoring grid using online scoreboard software,* or a simple Excel spreadsheet, here is what you should use that scoreboard to do:

1. ***Track high-priority KPIs.*** Verify that the KPIs your team chooses to track reflect the priorities of your customers, whether they are internal, external, or other stakeholder groups.
2. ***Capture.*** Capture feedback to identify purposeful actions and behaviors that will serve as the leading indicators for those high-priority KPIs.
3. ***Record.*** Record the actions and behaviors together with the names of the employees who will be working together to execute these leading indicators.
4. ***Communicate.*** Share these priorities at least daily, preferably multiple times each day.
5. ***Track purposeful actions and behaviors.*** Ask employees to report the frequency with which they perform

---

* Online scoreboards offer customizable tracking and reporting software that can support hundreds of users. It can be used on a PC, TV, smartphone, tablet, or any device that has a browser and is connected to the internet. Digital scoreboards can even be customized with company colors, logos, or profile images. These are ideal for those working in a virtual environment where it's not possible to huddle around a physical whiteboard.

these actions and behaviors. Note: These numbers are intended to be *directionally accurate*, generally correct, but not precise in terms of numbers, and to recognize total team contributions (read more on this below).

6. *Measure.* Tabulate the total frequency with which each listed action or behavior (leading indicator) was performed during the time period indicated.

7. *Correlate.* Assess whether there is a relationship between total team frequency of purposeful actions and behaviors (leading indicators) and improvement of KPIs (lagging indicators).

8. *Evaluate.* Critique results. Celebrate successes and learn from setbacks. Be prepared to adapt your approach by incorporating stakeholder feedback. Question assumptions and substitute purposeful actions and behaviors as needed.

You will find that the act of reflecting on which purposeful actions and behaviors likely correlate with the achievement of high-priority KPIs alone will increase the frequency of those actions and behaviors. The beauty of the reporting system is that, now, good intentions are being recorded as actual behavior. And the consistency with which they are performed can be correlated with the achievement of KPIs and progress toward the team's aspirational goal.

With a scoring grid like the example in figure 9, you are looking for directionally accurate numbers that will indicate progress and create momentum toward the team's aspirational goal. Obsessively precise recordkeeping is not recommended. It shouldn't be busy work. Keeping the grid up to date should not require employees to unnaturally stop what they're doing to tally an action or behavior on the whiteboard. The intent is to treat people like adults and not second-guess their self-reported figures. Admit up front to staff that self-reported figures should be as precise as possible, while also acknowledging that the realities of the workplace won't always allow them to stop what they're doing and tabulate an action or behavior.

Recognition in the workplace is a great thing. Frankly, there's not enough of it. Any device you can use, including this one, to increase the frequency with which you promote the contributions of your team members is a good idea. That said, the objective of this particular scoring grid is to recognize team, not individual, performance. Remember, the data is meant to be only directionally accurate; it likely will not be precise enough to evaluate individual performance.

Much as I appreciate the benefits of competition and accountability, scoring mechanisms that reward some people at the expense of others invite cynicism and tampering—both of which inhibit engagement. That's why my suggestion is to design a scoring system that tallies individual contributions while celebrating team performance. Think about the last time you either went bowling or played mini golf with your family or friends. Reflect on the collective enthusiasm you could have generated by tracking a team score. Even if you rolled a gutter ball or botched the windmill hole, your group could still have set a record score. It works the same way with this scoreboard. Individual progress is recorded, but the collective results are what will ultimately impact progression toward the team's objectives.

This doesn't mean that you can't offer a compliment or a word of affirmation to an employee who appears to be "outperforming" their peers in terms of production. The reality is that, as an accessible, visible, and engaged manager, you will know without consulting the scoring grid which of your team members is consistently practicing the purposeful actions and behaviors emphasized.

Note that the set of sample Actions and Behaviors and Results scoring grids are not intended to be prescriptive. There is nothing sacrosanct about the way I have formatted them. Your scoring grids may look very different. You may choose to combine the Actions and Behaviors tabulation grid with the Results grid rather than present them separately. And you may choose to reformat the reporting scheme and layout to suit your business and priorities. Adapt it to your needs. Make it your own. What is important is that your reporting system

- is highly visible to your employees
- lists a variety of high-value actions and behaviors (leading indicators) for employees to choose from that have the potential to influence KPIs and the team's aspirational goal
- links these actions and behaviors to KPIs and the team's aspirational goal (lagging indicators)
- enables you to track and measure in as close to real time as possible (update relentlessly)

Identify the criteria, timeframes, and layout that work best for your team and display the grid prominently. It is important for employee engagement to keep the scoreboard front and center and, with that, to keep job purpose top of mind. If this information is concealed in a folder and only shared periodically at meetings, it will do little to inspire daily performance, camaraderie, or collective aspirations. Do you want team members to always be thinking about their purpose at work and the actions and behaviors that reflect that purpose, making progress toward the team's aspirational goal, and pondering how their ongoing efforts influence critical KPIs? Do you want to make the team's contributions visible so that they can be celebrated often? Do you want to create accountability, a feeling that what they do matters, and a belief that they're making a difference together? Do you want to keep them engaged so they will want to continually aim higher? Get this scoreboard in front of your people and interact with it daily.

MAKING YOUR OWN SCORING GRID

In the far-left column of figure 9 are employee names followed by columns denoting each of the purposeful actions and behaviors the

ACTIONS/BEHAVIORS (8/23–29)						
NAME	APPROACH	OFFER NAME	15x5	REWARDS/ ENROLL	CARD/APP	TOTAL
Mark	20	20	30	5	5	80
Clara	21	18	25	7	2	73
Hakim	14	10	10	1	0	35
Beth	7	5	15	3	1	31
Maria	16	12	24	9	7	68
Aiyanna	23	22	31	5	5	86
Sam	17	12	15	4	0	48
Ajay	22	14	15	11	10	72
Ana	13	11	10	4	1	39
Jean	27	25	25	15	12	104
Ali	19	14	14	7	5	59
Liz	17	15	20	12	8	72
TOTALS	216	178	234	83	56	767

Figure 9: Actions and Behaviors Tally Grid

team has identified as leading indicators for the KPIs they are aiming to influence. There is no need to limit the purposeful actions and behaviors to those listed. There are an infinite number of actions and behaviors that employees can exhibit in support of job purpose. The ones on the board have simply been identified as the most likely levers (leading indicators) to influence the targeted KPIs.

A retailer's strategic objective is never simply to enroll a customer in a loyalty program; it's to activate that customer to engage in behaviors that reflect brand loyalty. It's the same with managing the performance of internal customers. The strategic objective should not be for employees to parrot lines like "Can I have your email address?" or "You can save 20 percent on today's purchase by applying for a rewards card." These lines typify a routine and transactional service experience. Chances are high that the customer heard the same set of robotic questions posed to the customer ahead of them in line. The strategic objective should be for employees to

RESULTS						
KPI	PERIOD ACTUAL	PERIOD GOAL	DIFFERENCE	YTD	2022 GOAL	DIFFERENCE
1. Overall satisfaction	88	90	(2)	88	90	(2)
2. Customer effort score	70	75	(5)	72	75	(3)
3. Net promoter score	57	60	(3)	58	60	(2)
4. Total sales	870,000	900,000	(30,000)	7,128,000	10,800,000	(3,672,000)
5. Intent to return	77	80	(3)	78	80	(2)
6. Intent to recommend	78	80	(2)	78	80	(2)
7. Customers' enrollment in loyalty program	332	400	(68)	2,765	4,800	(2,035)
8. Customers' application for store credit card	224	200	+24	1,435	2,400	(965)

Figure 10: Results Scoring Grid

make an authentic connection with customers by exhibiting purposeful actions and behaviors that will create progress toward the team's priorities (KPIs and aspirational goal).

Figure 10 depicts these KPIs in the far-left column followed by columns that display actual scores, goals, differences, and year-to-date results. The figures that are self-reported on the Actions and Behaviors scoring grid can be transferred to the Results grid by management. Either way, they must be kept current daily, with actions and behaviors being recorded shortly after they occur. If these scoring grids are allowed to languish and reports fall days or weeks behind because the focus shifts to job functions, then all you have is another failed quality campaign for employees to view with cynicism.

Don't be afraid to track sales and other revenue-related KPIs. A lot of purpose-driven thinking suggests "purpose over profit." What they mean is to not be so myopically focused on profit that you miss opportunities to honor your corporate mission, vision, purpose, and values. Organizations still need to measure financial performance. And that's okay. Profit is a worthy pursuit. Just don't become so consumed with it that your corporate ideals are marginalized.

In a 2020 interview, Hubert Joly, former Best Buy chairman and CEO, addressed a focus on profit: "There is a broad-based realization that an excessive focus on profits is wrong. It's of course the easiest thing to measure. There are generally accepted accounting principles [GAAP]. And at the end of each month, you know what your profit is. The problem is that if you focus too much on this outcome, you're going to be tempted to do the wrong thing. And, by the way, anybody who believes that your GAAP numbers, even your non-GAAP numbers, are a good measure of the economic value creation for a business, is wrong."[1]

He recommends a holistic approach to measuring performance: "I think the key in leading companies is to have a balanced scorecard, to have KPIs that are focused on customers, like a customer-satisfaction score or revenue per customer; on employee engagement and turnover; on vendors and how the relationship with them is going; your impact on and reputation in the community; *and* on financial performance."[2]

My goal is for you to identify the actions, behaviors, goals, and KPIs that will allow your scoreboard to be an awareness tool (to keep the focus on job purpose and the team's aspirational goal), a performance management tool (to validate progress and make midcourse corrections as needed), and an engagement tool (to celebrate successes and keep employees motivated). Remember that regardless of the results, there is always something to celebrate, even if you must be creative in identifying it.

It's true that in a retail setting, you can put marketing collateral in each customer's bag that promotes the store's loyalty program. Or you can simply print invitations to apply for the store's rewards credit card on customer receipts. Doing so would certainly eliminate the need to identify job purpose, have ongoing Revelation Conversations with your team, and to track purposeful actions and behaviors. If you're looking to be efficient in the way your organization promotes its loyalty program or credit card offers, marketing collateral and promotional receipts are the way to go. But if your goal is effectiveness, it's better to identify, track, measure, and correlate purposeful actions and behaviors aimed at these objectives.

NOT A (COMPLETELY) DEMOCRATIC PROCESS

Up until this point in the book, much of the counsel has required the leader or manager to make decisions with respect to answering the Four Questions, initiating the Revelation Conversation, and creating a scoring mechanism to encourage participation in practicing purposeful actions and behaviors (the leading indicators) that can influence the team's aims and objectives (the lagging indicators). It's crucial to recognize that not everything needs to be (or should be) a democratic process involving the opinions of numerous stakeholders.

As the leadership expert Patrick Lencioni wrote, "Values initiatives have nothing to do with building consensus—they are about imposing a set of fundamental, strategically sound beliefs on a broad group of people. Most executives understand the danger of consensus-driven decision-making when it comes to strategy, finance, and other business issues, yet they seem oblivious to the problem when it comes to developing values. Surveying all employees about what values they believe the company should adopt is a bad idea for two reasons. First, it integrates suggestions from many employees who probably don't belong at the company in the first place. And second, it creates the false impression that all input is equally valuable."[3]

Customers want to do business with organizations whose purpose and core values resonate with them. That's great, but let's be clear: Organizations must articulate an authentic purpose and a set of values and let the chips fall where they may with respect to customers that will or will not be attracted to those ideals. Organizations must be true to their principles, which are timeless and do not change, as opposed to reacting to the whims of customers' changing values and priorities.

There are, however, aspects of the process where I do recommend you involve employees and other stakeholders: the identification of KPIs and purposeful actions and behaviors. The KPIs will be more relevant to the needs of those impacted by them, and employees will feel more committed to the purposeful actions and behaviors they themselves propose. And since frontline employees are closer to customers, they have unique insight into obstacles and opportunities that management may lack.

Before you select high-priority KPIs and the leading indicators that have the potential to influence them, check in with your customers—internal and external—who are affected by the KPIs, actions, and behaviors you've chosen. If you have five KPIs, rank them in order of importance. I bet if you survey your customers, their ranking will differ. And this assumes you chose the five highest-value KPIs, which may or may not be the case. Maybe your company's top priority is its net promoter score, which is an indication of customer loyalty, but your customers' top priority is customer effort score, which is an indication of how much effort they must exert to purchase or return a product, or to get an issue resolved, a request fulfilled, or a question answered.

The fact is, most decisions about KPIs and process improvement steps are made inside the company, with little, if any, input from customers. Sure, some sophisticated companies survey their customers, but they frequently bastardize the process through poor execution, undermining its value. Don't miss this valuable opportunity to collect feedback to make your employees' work more purposeful. Many companies produce lengthy surveys and realize abysmal response rates. If you want customers to respond and do so thoughtfully, limit your surveys to five to seven key questions that you plan to do something about rather than ten, twenty, or thirty questions whose responses will be ignored or never acted upon.

After you have identified a lagging indicator (such as a KPI) that you want to influence, you will want to examine the processes that contribute to that metric. For instance, if the KPI is value for price paid, then you will want to get stakeholder input pertaining to ways that value can be added to the process of delivering a particular product or service. Especially for products and services that have a price premium, identifying ways to add value can reduce consumers' price resistance.

One popular way to add value is by offering a *lagniappe*, a Louisiana French term for something given as a small, unexpected gift, such as a complimentary bottle of water at a car dealership, hand lotion samples as are provided at L'Occitane en Provence, or a trial-size packet of ground coffee beans from Starbucks. Value can also be delivered in the form of cleanliness, friendliness, or speed. Are you willing to go out of your way to pay more for an experience at a supermarket, convenience store, or coffee shop that is cleaner, has friendlier employees, or provides faster service? Most consumers are.

According to research from PwC, 86 percent of buyers are willing to pay more for a great customer experience. The more expensive the item, the more they are willing to pay. For example, customers are willing to pay a price premium of up to 13 percent (and as high as 18 percent) for luxury and indulgence services, simply by receiving a great customer experience.[4]

There are a variety of sources of feedback to help identify those actions and behaviors that may improve your KPIs. Once identified, the key is to act on them and keep these efforts center stage. The scoring grids are one effective way to do so. Another, as I'll discuss in the next chapter, is igniting team spirit with a rallying cry.

Exercise

Identify a single key performance indicator for an internal customer, external customer, or other stakeholder group that could benefit from a renewed focus. Next, identify one to three purposeful actions or behaviors (leading indicators) that have the potential to positively influence that KPI (a lagging indicator).

Note: This is just an exercise to get the ball rolling. In your real world of work, beware of determining these priorities in a vacuum. It's vital that you compare your assumptions about what the true priorities are with what your customers, other stakeholders, and data points are telling you.

KEY PERFORMANCE INDICATOR TO BE ADDRESSED:

_____

LEADING INDICATORS

Purposeful action or behavior 1:

_____

Purposeful action or behavior 2:

_____

Purposeful action or behavior 3:

_____

7 | Creating Team Alignment

R ival groups of fifth-grade campers that had been sworn enemies were now being forced to work together to solve a common problem. With the July sun beating down and their canteens dry, the only water supply to the isolated campground had stopped flowing.

Two weeks earlier, in June 1954, twenty-two boys arrived at the Robbers Cave State Park campground in Oklahoma on two separate buses, unaware of the existence of the other group. They were also oblivious to the fact that they were participants in an experiment led by the social psychologist Muzafer Sherif. He and his team posed as camp counselors to observe the emergence of social norms, leadership hierarchies, and group structure and to document how the groups would respond to competition and, later, the need to work toward a shared goal.

During the first week of camp, the two groups of eleven campers hiked, swam, ate, and slept independent from the other group. That changed in the second week, when the campers were brought together to compete in a tournament. Each camp designed a flag emblazoned with its name, the Eagles and the Rattlers. The competitions included baseball, tug-of-war, touch football, and tent pitching, with the winning camp earning trophies, medals, and prized folding pocketknives.

With the declaration of a winning and a losing camp, aggression surfaced in the form of name-calling and vandalism—including the burning of each camp's flag. Fistfights broke out between members of opposing camps. Rival cabins were ransacked and looted.

And then the water stopped.

Members of the Eagles and Rattlers now had to work together to inspect the milelong water pipe, find the blockage, and make the repair. With the water once again flowing to the campground, spirits lifted. There was a sense of accomplishment, camaraderie, and mutual respect. Later, members of both camps agreed to share a single bus ride home. And when boys from the Eagles were short on money during the trip, the Rattlers paid for their malt beverages.

In the Robbers Cave experiment, Dr. Sherif and his team succeeded in artificially building up mutual aggression between two groups of campers and observed that the hostility subsided only when the boys dedicated themselves to a common purpose. Faced with a superordinate goal, one that both camps cared about and would need to work together to achieve, the Eagles and Rattlers united as one camp.[1]

This story encapsulates what managers deal with every day. Although it may not devolve into name-calling, sabotage, or fistfights, managers do face conflict. They encounter obstacles, even crises, that require empathy, flexibility, and creativity to resolve. They are expected to model and foster a culture of trust, mutual respect, and camaraderie. They have opportunities to recognize and celebrate desired performance. They are looked to for leadership and professional development as they align employees in the collective pursuit of a common aspirational goal.

Alignment precedes progress, momentum, and sustainment. Lack of alignment is the Achilles' heel of corporate improvement campaigns, specifically, a lack of alignment between the priorities, expectations, and resources of leadership and those of various stakeholders. As the leadership expert Jim Collins notes, "Building a visionary company requires one percent vision and 99 percent alignment."[2]

Too many teams at work are not actually teams at all. They are work groups toiling together until the end of another uninspiring shift. As in the Robbers Cave experiment, independent "camps" form, territories are set, pecking orders are established, and mindsets are fixed. Competition and breached territorial lines create conflict, at least until a crisis produces a superordinate goal that aligns the camps in a unified pursuit of a resolution.

As the educational psychologist Bruce Tuckman originally proposed in 1965, some phases of group development are necessary and inevitable for a team to grow. Although there have been variations and enhancements to Tuckman's work over the years, "forming, storming, norming, and performing" still provides a useful framework for team development.[3] Each of these phases was evident in the Robbers Cave experiment. Two work groups (camps, in this case) came together (forming phase). They initially experienced conflict as expectations aligned (storming phase). Then they began to settle into predicable routines (norming phase), and, eventually, achieved a common goal (performing phase).

Think about your own work group as being in the forming phase, coming together around a new way to view their job roles and connect their daily responsibilities to job purpose. There will be resistance to your ideas and any new protocols introduced, as is the case with most initiatives that nudge people out of their comfort zone. That storming phase will be followed by a period of stability as covenants are accepted and standards are recognized in the norming phase. Next, the magic happens.

The fourth phase, performing, is where all the effort, discomfort, and vulnerability that went into trying something different begins to pay off. It might be tentative at first as an employee asks a question in a follow-up to the Revelation Conversation. Or an employee might offer a suggestion for a purposeful action that could be adopted by the team as a leading indicator for the Actions and Behaviors scoring grid. Maybe an employee makes a comment or poses a question that indicates curiosity about an element of the Results scoring grid. In other words, they begin to see an alignment between their jobs, their goals, their team members, and the collective effort required to succeed.

As team members align, receptivity and interest increase. More questions are asked. More observations and comments are made. Participation increases. With participation comes team commitment and spirit. With team spirit comes full team engagement. And wherever there is full team engagement, results are sure to follow.

The improvement programs that I have seen succeed have not only leadership support but also a credible program champion who aligns the interests of all stakeholders with the higher purpose of the effort. They also tend to start small, often with a single work group, and are highly visible despite their initial small scale. As a result of early successes, these programs tend to gain momentum, attract interest, and expand. Employees who are engaged in these initiatives tend to exhibit enthusiasm and commitment in their work and workplace.

But like the phases of group development, it's not possible to circumvent the process of aligning employees and fostering team spirit. As the leader, you must do the yeoman's work to build a foundation from which camaraderie, mutual trust, and support spring. In the context of the Revelation Conversation, that means becoming familiar with the three parts of every job role: job knowledge, job skills, and job purpose. It calls for you to be fluent in organizational purpose and committed to initiating ongoing conversations about job purpose, values, and purposeful actions and behaviors with your team. It requires that you identify and champion an aspirational goal in support of that purpose.

You must do the ongoing work required to keep job purpose top of mind and visible. You must identify, track, and promote the purposeful actions and behaviors that have the potential to positively impact key performance indicators (KPIs), quotas, budgets and other metrics. After all, performance cannot be quantified without measurement and results cannot be seen without posting them. Correlations cannot be made without determining the relationship between the variables. And enthusiasm for the shared pursuit of a common aspirational goal cannot be stoked without frequent check-ins and celebration of the team's progress. You will know that your engagement efforts are successful when you feel a palpable team spirit, what the French call *esprit de corps*, bubbling up during meetings and even chance encounters with individual team members.

ESPRIT DE CORPS:
THE HOLY GRAIL OF ENGAGEMENT

My son Cooper, now in college, has played competitive basketball most of his life. One early team Cooper joined was led by an outstanding head coach who is a former Division 1 student-athlete and a retired NFL linebacker. As a former professional athlete competing at the highest level in sports, Coach Terrence speaks with authority. I especially appreciate the attention he paid to camaraderie and what it meant for the boys to be selfless and a part of something bigger than themselves.

During each practice, the boys would line up beneath the goal behind the baseline while each member of the team was called out, one at a time, to the free throw line to take two shots. Rather than convey indifference by talking among themselves while awaiting their turn to shoot or, worse, chiding their teammates for missed baskets, the boys had been instructed to approach the shooter, make eye contact, slap hands, and offer verbal encouragement using the teammate's name after each shot—regardless of whether a basket was made.

To me, it is the perfect representation of esprit de corps—a feeling of pride, fellowship, and common loyalty toward one another. The first time I witnessed this, I considered what would happen if more managers followed Coach Terrence's example in the workplace. Divisive, territorial cliques and posturing would be eschewed in favor of congeniality and support, subordinating criticism to encouragement, and even offering high fives every now and then.

THE RALLYING CRY

While directing the 1956 epic film *The Ten Commandments*, Cecil B. DeMille, frustrated by the lack of enthusiasm displayed by a large group of extras portraying the Israelites, challenged them to energize their performance, shouting, "All right now. Give me everything you've got, people! Don't be extras. Be a nation!"[4]

Clearly, the extras responded. The film was nominated for seven Academy Awards, including best picture, and was the most financially successful film in 1956.[5] DeMille's dilemma reflects the ongoing challenge facing leaders to inspire employees, many of whom regularly display their indifference by simply going through the motions at work, disconnected from job purpose. Their "performances" are uninspired—lacking energy, enthusiasm, and commitment.

Think about the attributes of successful improvement programs. In addition to leadership support, they have a credible program champion (that's you) who aligns the interests of all stakeholders; they start small and expand; and they are highly visible. Oh, and there's one more element that can support your efforts to further alignment and inspire esprit de corps: create a compelling rallying cry.

Too often, corporate quality campaigns or improvement initiatives fail to capture the hearts and minds of employees. The beauty of a rallying cry is in its simplicity and ability to unite employees in the collective pursuit of a shared goal.

Whether or not we possess DeMille's commanding presence or megaphone through which to communicate expectations and implore excellence, we all have the capacity to reinforce standards, amplify the goal, and spur performance using a credible, inspiring rallying cry.

The hardest part of developing a relevant and sustainable rallying cry is the preparation required to capture the essence of your organization's character and articulate team members' job purpose. This labor must occur well before the fun work of crafting a team rallying cry begins. Hopefully, if you've gotten this far into the book, you've already done the work, first by answering the Four Questions posed in chapter 3 and second, by initiating Revelation Conversations with your employees to reveal and operationalize job purpose.

Rallying Cry-teria

A rallying cry (also known as a credo, motto, mantra, or anthem) "is a short, simple phrase that encapsulates the beliefs and ambitions that guide an individual or organization. . . . [These] mottos spark within us the internal fortitude to press forward through tough decisions and overwhelming opposition."[6]

There is an ambitious element to a rallying cry; the ambition needs to be tied to your organization's character and aligned with job purpose, values, and the team's aspirational goal. In many cases, your response to the question, "What is my team's aspirational goal?" (question 4 in chapter 3) will closely resemble your team's rallying cry. But a rallying cry is not a slogan or tagline. While in some cases it can be both (e.g., Apple's "Think Different" or Bombas's "Bee Better"), in most cases it will be internal and used to rally employees, not customers.

Here are my criteria for an inspiring, purposeful rallying cry. It should be

- simple
- short and easy to remember
- actionable (starts with a verb)
- connected to mission, vision, purpose
- inspirational
- credible

A Rallying Cry Is Simple

As the journalist Elizabeth Bernstein put it, "Modern mantras are ... effective because they're repetitive and simple, making them easy to turn into a habit. We don't have to search for the positive thought to call up; we already have it."[7]

An article in the *New Yorker* that profiled the late musician Bill Withers referenced a hit from his 1971 album, *Just as I Am*: "'Ain't No Sunshine' is a two-minute song with only three verses, a bridge that repeats two words twenty-six times—'I know'—and no chorus to speak of. Withers likes to form guitar chords that he can simply move up and down the neck without altering the position of his fingers. This simple approach leaves room for his baritone voice to map out subtle, articulate melodies."[8]

"Ain't No Sunshine" gave Withers his first gold record, earned him a Grammy, and, with its timeless appeal, contributed significantly to his lifetime royalties. This success resulted from Withers's "simple approach" to songwriting.

A Rallying Cry Is Short and Easy to Remember

A rallying cry should consist of no more than two to five words. There may be exceptions, but shorter will always be better—the best rallying cries can be absorbed without reading them. Improvement efforts often struggle for relevance, time, and attention in the weeks and months following their introduction. They are like New Year's resolutions, whether related to physical or financial health, that fade from our consciousness before Super Bowl Sunday. That's why being punchy and easy to recall is key.

Put up all your rallying cry candidates onto a whiteboard or flip chart and try to eliminate every possible word that doesn't add value or clarify meaning. Try to consolidate words, too, combining words and seeing where you can use, for example, two words in place of three.

A play on words can also be appealing and memorable. Consider MD Anderson Cancer Center's "Make Cancer History" and the campaign hashtag of outdoor retailer Recreation Equipment Inc. (REI) promoting an alternative to Black Friday mayhem: "#OptOutside." (More on REI below.)

A Rallying Cry Is Actionable

The best rallying cries are pithy and action oriented. Some examples: "Save lives" (Grail); "Beat yesterday" (Garmin); "Carpe momentum," which translates as "seize the moment" or "Carpe diem," which brings to mind the scene in *Dead Poets Society* when the English teacher John Keating (actor Robin Williams) leans into the boys and whispers, "Carpe diem. Seize the day, boys. Make your lives extraordinary." And the original battle cry of the Almogavars (fourteenth-century Spanish warriors), "Desperta ferro!" (Awake, iron!). And one more that's better in Latin: Ite, inflammate omnia! (Go, set the world on fire!). This rallying cry was used by Ignatius of Loyola, a sixteenth-century Catholic priest, to inspire missionaries to spread the word of God.[9]

Notice all the verbs? Pretty compelling—and all three words or less.

A Rallying Cry Is Connected to Mission, Vision, Purpose

Patagonia's mission is "We're in business to save our home planet." When the federal government ordered the reduction of two national monuments in Utah in 2017, Patagonia decided to make the protection of the public land its business agenda. Patagonia replaced its website homepage with a new webpage stating its stance on this issue and a path for consumers to donate to the cause.[10] If I were a team leader at Patagonia, the rallying cry for my team might be

"Save our home planet!" or, even shorter, "Save Earth!" Based on the company's actions in support of its mission, such a rallying cry would be natural for team members to adopt.

Consider pharmacy giant CVS Health. Its purpose statement reads: "Bringing our heart to every moment of your health." It even has a heart in its company logo. In 2014, CVS Health discontinued the sale of tobacco products at its US retail locations, forfeiting billions of dollars in revenue. At the time, the company's CEO said, "Put simply, the sale of tobacco products is inconsistent with our purpose."[11] Given its focus on health, an effective rallying cry for the company's employees could be "Health is everything!"*

A Rallying Cry Is Inspirational

Outdoor retailer REI has a core purpose that reads, "To inspire, educate and outfit for a lifetime of outdoor adventure and stewardship." Every year since 2015, REI has closed all its stores on Black Friday, the busiest retail day of the year, to give employees a paid day off to enjoy the outdoors with friends and family. The name of this campaign, #OptOutside, also serves as an inspirational rallying cry for employees and other stakeholders. According to the company's website, "#OptOutside is more than a day—it's been our way of life as a co-op since 1938. REI is committed to helping people tap into the joy, renewal and connection that comes from spending time outside with friends and family, and we see Black Friday as a perfect time to do this."[12] In addition to demonstrating the company's commitment to putting purpose before profits, the campaign has inspired more than seven hundred organizations to join the movement.

Inspirational is good but hackneyed is bad—you know, tired phrases like "Reach for the stars" or "The A-team" or "We are the

---

* It's true that this rallying cry does not start with a verb. That's okay. Chapter 2 contains the example "Absolute Customer Satisfaction!" which begins with an adjective. And perhaps the best-known rallying cry, Nike's "Just do it," starts with an adverb. So there are options.

champions" or "Best of the best." These phrases are so overused as to inspire little interest or attention. It's also important not to put "inspiration" before substance, as I explain next.

A Rallying Cry Is Credible

Tell the truth with your rallying cry. It must be credible, believable, authentic, and convincing if it is to genuinely inspire and endure. Avoid exaggerated or hyperbolic expressions and superlatives like best, biggest, or greatest. If you're too over the top, your rallying cry may be viewed with skepticism.

Commemorate It

Anything you can do to commemorate a rallying cry will aid in its visibility and retention—whether it's posters in the lunchroom, logoed swag, or unexpected gifts to team members.

Though silicone wristbands may lack the novelty they had in 2004, when the iconic yellow Livestrong bracelet campaign launched, they are a great example of commemorating a rallying cry. They are proximate (right there on your wrist) and visible (bright yellow) and thus serve as a constant reminder of one's commitment to the cause, in this case, supporting those affected by cancer. The sock company Bombas commemorates its commitment to mission and purpose by sewing its mantra "Bee Better" into its socks and printing it on the interior of its T-shirts.

Commemorating is a tactic I also use in my own work. After collaborating with a client in Rhode Island to certify a dozen in-house customer service trainers, I sent each person a brass pineapple desk ornament as a physical reminder of their commitment to hospitality. Fun fact: Dating back to colonial America, the pineapple has served as a symbol of hospitality and warm welcome.

MOTIVATION VERSUS INSPIRATION

Two terms that often foster debate are motivate and inspire. Are people motivated to perform well or are they inspired to do so?

Although some take exception to the term *motivate*, contending that people cannot be motivated but rather motivate themselves, the literal definition of the word is *to stimulate someone's interest in or enthusiasm for doing something*. So, even though the behavior is up to the individual, managers can motivate or stimulate their interest or enthusiasm for exhibiting desired behavior.

Similarly, the word *inspire* literally means *to fill someone with the urge or ability to do or feel something*. Again, managers can't make people feel inspired. That's up to them. But they can create an environment, through words and actions, that fills people with the urge or ability to feel something and to act on those feelings. If you've ever been moved by a compelling speech or video, then you know what I mean.

Here's my favorite story about motivating—or inspiring—behavior. It is adapted from a recorded speech that I listened to many years ago by the late educator and motivational speaker Dr. Kenneth McFarland.[13] The story illustrates the point that, regardless of whether someone is *motivated* or *inspired*, it is ultimately up to the individual to take action, to exhibit desired behaviors, and to realize their potential.

There was a young man who worked the late shift and always walked home afterward. On one particularly moonlit night, he discovered a shortcut that took him through the local cemetery.

He repeated the route for several nights while the moon continued to light a path. The next night, although the moonlight waned, he was confident that he could find his way through the dark cemetery. As he retraced his steps from the night before, he fell into a deep grave that had been dug earlier that day. After numerous failed attempts to scale the dirt walls, he resigned himself to spending the night alone in the grave.

He was seated in a darkened corner of the grave, half-asleep, when another late-night traveler happened to stumble into the pit. After listening to the other's unsuccessful attempts to escape, the young man said, "Friend, you can't get out of here."

But he did—on his very next try!

Now, that's motivation!

ALIGNMENT ALWAYS COMES FIRST

Musicians are often used to illustrate the epitome of cooperation, actively working together as a unit toward the same result—literally, to be in harmony as they produce beautiful music. If you find yourself at the symphony, notice that the musicians play a few notes just before the concert begins.

Before the conductor takes the stage to lead the orchestra, the musicians need to be certain that their instruments are perfectly in tune with one another. To accomplish this, the concertmaster stands up and asks for quiet. After the audience falls silent, the oboe plays an A as a tuning note into an electronic tuner and all the musicians play that same note to hear if they are exactly in tune.

Musicians with string instruments adjust their A string, followed by the remaining strings of their instrument as needed. Wind players also adjust their instruments accordingly. The reason the oboe plays the tuning note is partly tradition and partly because its sound is penetrating.[14]

In the same way, if they are to accomplish or make progress toward their goals, team members need to be on the same page with respect to their purpose, values, and aspirational goal. A rallying cry is an effective way to combat the siren call of job functions and keep the entire team aligned and focused on their higher purpose.

The goal of all group development efforts is progression from one phase of group development to the next, culminating in high performance. The same is true for improvement efforts. There is a place to start and a sequence to follow before achieving an objective or making progress toward team goals. Most corporate quality programs fail, or at least fail to deliver on the original program objectives. The preeminent cause of this failure, other than leadership indifference, is a misalignment of priorities, expectations, and resources. Alignment precedes progress.

In addition to the attributes of successful improvement programs (e.g., leadership support, having a credible program champion who aligns the interests of all stakeholders, starting small and then expanding, and being highly visible), creating a team rallying cry can support your efforts to further team alignment, heighten program visibility, inspire esprit de corps, foster camaraderie, and maintain the focus on the team's aspirational goal.

The activity below can help you to succeed where others have failed.

Exercise

1. DEVELOP A RALLYING CRY

Recall the aspirational goal you identified for your team in chapter 3. Is it a candidate to become the team's rallying cry as is? (As stated earlier, it is imperative that leadership drives this process. If you determine that your team's aspirational goal already fits the criteria for your team's rallying cry, then there is no need to vote on it.) You are the leader. If you don't think the aspirational goal is appropriate as a rallying cry, use it as the basis for developing one together with your team using the "rallying cry-teria" listed in this chapter.

2. COMMEMORATE IT

Citizens of a nation connect to its flag and national anthem. Family members connect to their family crest. Students and alumni connect to school colors, mascots, and fight songs. In the Robbers Cave experiment, each camp chose a name and designed a flag to signify its identity. Professional sports teams do the same via colors, mascots, and stadium chants.

Invite team members to participate in a creative process that will culminate in a poster, mural, logo, icon, or coat of arms that symbolizes your team's aspirations and commitment. Choose significant colors, images, symbols, and words that are associated with the organization and are meaningful to the team.

3. USE IT

In the 2015 Sugar Bowl, the Alabama Crimson Tide led the Ohio State Buckeyes 21–6 midway through the second quarter before Ohio State went on a 28–0 run to take a 34–21 lead late in the third quarter. Top-ranked Alabama's collapse contributed to a premature end to its season, losing to the fourth-ranked Buckeyes who went on to defeat the Oregon Ducks in the national title game.

The following season, Alabama lived by the mantra "Finish."[15] This rallying cry was not merely posted on bulletin boards and referenced now and then by the coaching staff or in team meetings. It was incorporated daily into the athletes' real world of work: conditioning, preparation, and execution. Athletes were challenged to *finish* reps in the weight room, *finish* plays during practice, and *finish* scoring drives in games. And the ultimate goal was to *finish* the season as national champions.

On January 11, 2016, Alabama met Clemson in the 2016 College Football Playoff National Championship, winning the game 45–40. By rallying around the concept of refusing to do anything halfway, the team did, in fact, *finish* the season as national champions.

Conclusion:
Start with One

In December 2020, my thirteen-year-old son Carter told me about a man he had seen on social media who was doing hundreds of push-ups each day. This was a daunting feat to consider until Carter added that this person began doing daily push-ups a couple of years earlier, starting with a single push-up and then adding one per day.

Carter explained that the push-ups weren't consecutive; they were spread out in sets throughout the day. The goal was to complete the total number of push-ups in sets of ten, twenty, or whatever number seemed reasonable, over the course of the day. He challenged me to do the same by starting with a single push-up, adding a second push-up the following day, and so on.

By the end of December, I was up to 31 push-ups a day and as of May 26, 2021, the day I separated my right shoulder in a "parents versus athletes" whiffle ball game, I was up to 176 daily push-ups. (Don't feel sorry for me. I got a twelve-year-old out on the play.)

You probably already know where I'm going with this. Although initiating the Revelation Conversation with your entire staff may appear daunting, if you consider starting with a single member of your staff, it becomes more approachable. And take comfort in knowing that you won't be expected to hold Revelation Conversations daily or within any timeframe other than the one you set for yourself. The goal is to initiate a Revelation Conversation with each member of your staff, but the timing is up to you.

MINOR IMPROVEMENTS, MASSIVE RESULTS

The aggregation of marginal gains is a concept that was popularized by the British cycling coach Dave Brailsford, who was featured in the book, *Atomic Habits*, by James Clear.[1]

Coach Brailsford was hired in 2002 to improve the competitiveness of the British cycling team in international cycling competitions. "Since 1908, British riders had won just a single gold medal at the Olympic Games and they had fared even worse in cycling's biggest race, the Tour de France. In 110 years, no British cyclist had ever won the event."[2]

After assessing the situation, Coach Brailsford recalled the theory of marginal gains from his MBA program. "It struck me," he said, "that we should think small, not big, and adopt a philosophy of continuous improvement through the aggregation of marginal gains. Forget about perfection; focus on progression, and compound the improvements."[3]

With that, Brailsford and the team set out to identify and make incremental improvements in every aspect of cycling that had any opportunity for improvement—even a 1 percent opportunity—from cycling equipment, to riders' health and nutrition, to the color of the bike trailer's floor.

The team found tires that were a fraction lighter, seats that were slightly more comfortable, and cleaning methods that enabled them to locate and remove dust from hard-to-reach components of their bikes. The cyclists' nutrition was optimized for the physical demands of racing. The athletes used their own mattresses and pillows while traveling so they could sleep in the same posture every night. A surgeon was hired to teach team members the most effective way to wash their hands to minimize the chances of getting sick. And handshakes were forbidden during international competitions for the same reason. No detail was too insignificant to consider. The floor of the team's bike trailer was painted white so they could more easily identify dust and remove it.

According to Coach Brailsford, "We searched for small improvements everywhere and found countless opportunities. Taken together, we felt they gave us a competitive advantage."[4]

Did it make a difference?

With only a single Olympic gold medal in its entire hundred-year history prior to 2008, the British cycling team won seven out of ten Olympic gold medals in track cycling at the 2008 Summer Olympic Games in Beijing. And four years later, at the 2012 Summer Olympic Games in London, they repeated the feat, winning seven out of ten Olympic gold medals in the sport. The team's dominance continued at the 2016 Summer Olympic Games in Rio de Janeiro, where they won six out of ten Olympic gold medals in track cycling.

In addition to Olympic glory, a member of the British cycling team won six out of seven Tour de France races between 2012 and 2018—a race that a British cyclist had never won before.

In *Atomic Habits*, Mr. Clear writes about the aggregation of marginal gains. "Too often, we convince ourselves that massive success requires massive action. Whether it is losing weight, building a business, writing a book, winning a championship, or achieving any other goal, we put pressure on ourselves to make some earth-shattering improvement that everyone will talk about.

"Meanwhile, improving by 1 percent isn't particularly notable—sometimes it isn't even *noticeable*—but it can be far more meaningful, especially in the long run. The difference a tiny improvement can make over time is astounding."[5]

If you take tiny steps to improve your performance by just 1 percent each day for one year, you can end up nearly 38 percent better according to the aggregation of marginal gains graph (1.01^{365} = 37.78), illustrated in figure 11.

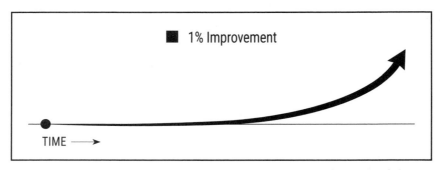

Figure 11: Aggregation of Marginal Gains

This is the result you would get if you did just 1 percent more than usual—or about five minutes more per day in an eight-hour workday. What if you invested that time to

- initiate the Revelation Conversation
- solicit ways to incorporate job essence into job function
- identify and track purposeful actions and behaviors that reflect job purpose and move KPIs
- develop and champion an aspirational goal
- create a rallying cry
- celebrate purpose-driven successes

In the summer of 1998, during a work trip to St. Louis, a colleague and I attended a baseball game at Busch Stadium between the St. Louis Cardinals and the Kansas City Royals. This was the summer that Mark McGwire and Sammy Sosa were chasing Roger Maris's regular season record of 61 home runs. McGwire hit his 37th home run of the season that night and went on to surpass Maris's longstanding record, ending the season at 70.[6] What a feat!

You would expect that the Cardinals would have clinched their division that season or possibly even competed in the World Series, but they finished third in the division with a record of 83–79 and did not even qualify for the playoffs.

Everyone was so consumed with McGwire's home runs that the focus shifted from getting base hits to "Big Mac's" next at bat. The home run leader on the World Series championship team that year was Tino Martinez of the New York Yankees, with 28 home runs—just 40 percent of McGwire's total.

If you're thinking big and always swinging for the fences, team performance can be spotty, and you just might find yourself in third place, two back from your goal.

As Dave Brailsford advised, "think small, not big." And as I recommend: start with one.

THE 90-DAY CHALLENGE

What if over the next 90 days you held a total of 90 informal five-minute one-on-one Revelation Conversations (either initial or follow-up conversations) with members of your team? What if within that timeframe you identified the KPIs that matter most to your customers and correlate with business success? What if you isolated and tracked the purposeful actions and behaviors that team members could exhibit in support of those objectives and their aspirational goal? What difference would you expect to see?

Would your team members feel more connected to their job roles? Would the frequency of their purposeful actions and behaviors increase? Would your target KPIs improve?

Try it for 90 days. My hunch is that, based on your results, you will commit to another 90-day challenge and so forth. Along the way, you will master your version of the Revelation Conversation and find ways to build on and improve every recommendation in this book.

Ite, inflammate omnia! (Go, set the world on fire!)

Notes

INTRODUCTION

1. Thomas Höge and Tatjana Schnell, "No Work Commitment without a Sense of Purpose. A Study on the Relationship between Work Engagement, Meaningfulness, and Job Characteristics," *Business Psychology* [in German] 1 (2012): 91–99.
2. A. M. Grant, "The Significance of Task Significance: Job Performance Effects, Relational Mechanisms, and Boundary Conditions," *Journal of Applied Psychology* 93, no. 1 (2008): 108–24, https://doi.org / 10.1037/0021-9010.93.1.108.
3. Gallup Inc., The Relationship between Engagement at Work and Organizational Outcomes, *2020 Q¹² Meta-Analysis*, 10th ed. (Washington, October 2020).
4. Steve Curtin, *Delight Your Customers: 7 Simple Ways to Raise Your Customer Service from Ordinary to Extraordinary* (New York: AMACOM–HarperCollins Leadership, 2013).
5. Simon Sinek, *Start with Why: How Great Leaders Inspire Everyone to Take Action* (New York: Portfolio, 2009).

CHAPTER 1

1. Louie Schwartzberg, "Finding Purpose in People: A Story by Norman Lear," *Moving Art* (blog), April 11, 2016, https://movingart.com /purpose-norman-lear/.
2. Shirley Musich et al., "Purpose in Life and Positive Health Outcomes among Older Adults," *Popular Health Management* 21, no. 2 (April 2018): 139–47, https://doi.org/10.1089/pop.2017.0063.

3. Rosemarie Kobau et al., "Well-Being Assessment: An Evaluation of Well-Being Scales for Public Health and Population Estimates of Well-Being among US Adults," *Applied Psychology: Health and Well-Being* 2, no. 3 (2010): 272–97, https://doi.org/10.1111/j.1758-0854.2010.01035.x.

4. Dhruv Khullar, "Finding Purpose for a Good Life, but Also a Healthy One," *New York Times*, January 1, 2018.

5. Arne Gast et al., "Purpose: Shifting from Why to How," *McKinsey Quarterly*, April 22, 2020.

6. Viktor E. Frankl, *Man's Search for Meaning* (Boston: Beacon Press, 2006), 85.

7. Frankl, *Man's Search for Meaning*, 106.

8. Abraham Maslow, "A Theory of Human Motivation," *Psychological Review* 50, no. 4 (1943): 370–96, http://dx.doi.org/10.1037/h0054346.

9. Derek Thompson, "Workism Is Making Americans Miserable," *The Atlantic*, February 24, 2019, https://www.theatlantic.com/ideas/archive/2019/02/religion-workism-making-americans-miserable/583441/.

10. Jim Harter, "U.S. Employee Engagement Holds Steady in First Half of 2021," Gallup Inc., July 29, 2021.

11. Gallup Inc., *State of the Global Workplace: 2021 Report* (Washington, DC, 2021).

12. Gallup Inc., "U.K. and Western Europe Have Least Engaged Employees Globally, Though Stress Levels Decreased During Pandemic," published by PR Newswire, June 9, 2021, https://www.prnewswire.co.uk/news-releases/u-k-and-western-europe-have-least-engaged-employees-globally-though-stress-levels-decreased-during-pandemic-872173470.html.

13. Jim Harter, "Historic Drop in Employee Engagement Follows Record Rise," *Gallup Workplace*, July 2, 2020, https://www.gallup.com/workplace/313313/historic-drop-employee-engagement-follows-record-rise.aspx.

14. Vipula Gandhi and Jennifer Robison, "The 'Great Resignation' Is Really the 'Great Discontent,'" Gallup Inc., July 22, 2021.

CHAPTER 2

1. Michael A. Fuoco, "Arrest in Bank Robbery, Suspect's TV Picture Spurs Tips," *Pittsburgh Post-Gazette*, March 21, 1996, 37.

2. Justin Kruger and David Dunning, "Unskilled and Unaware of It: How Difficulties in Recognizing One's Own Incompetence Lead to Inflated

Self-Assessments," *Journal of Personality and Social Psychology* 77, no. 6 (December 1999): 1121–34, https://doi.org/10.1037// 0022-3514.77.6.1121.

3. Mark Murphy, "The Dunning-Kruger Effect Shows Why Some People Think They're Great Even When Their Work Is Terrible," *Forbes*, January 24, 2017, https://www.forbes.com/sites/markmurphy/2017/01/24 /the-dunning-kruger-effect-shows-why-some-people-think-theyre -great-even-when-their-work-is-terrible/?sh=79bc18905d7c.

4. Credit Suisse Research Institute, *Global Wealth Report 2021* (Zurich, Switzerland, June 2021), 21.

5. Errol Morris, "The Anosognosic's Dilemma: Something's Wrong but You'll Never Know What It Is (Part 1)," *New York Times*, June 20, 2010.

6. Tom Connellan, *Inside the Magic Kingdom: Seven Keys to Disney's Success* (Austin, TX: Bard Press, 1996).

7. Morris, "Anosognosic's Dilemma."

8. Bruce Jones, "The Difference between Purpose and Mission," *Harvard Business Review*, February 2, 2016, https://hbr.org/sponsored/2016/02 /the-difference-between-purpose-and-mission.

9. Jones, "Purpose and Mission."

10. Jones, "Purpose and Mission."

11. Connellan, *Inside the Magic Kingdom*, 28–29.

CHAPTER 3

1. "Back to Africa," *The Zoo*, season 1, episode 8, Animal Planet, April 7, 2017.

2. "Back to Africa."

3. "Back to Africa."

4. "At LEGO, Growth and Culture Are Not Kid Stuff," Boston Consulting Group website, February 9, 2017, https://www.bcg.com /publications/2017/people-organization-jorgen-vig-knudstorp-lego -growth-culture-not-kid-stuff.

5. Carol Cone, "What Does a Purpose-Driven Company Look Like?," *Salesforce.com* (blog), July 18, 2019, https://www.salesforce.org/blog /what-does-a-purpose-driven-company-look-like/.

6. "Living Our Purpose," Kroger, http://krogerstories.com/living-our -purpose, accessed October 18, 2021.

7. Kantar Consulting, *Purpose 2020: The Journey towards Purpose-Led Growth* (London: May 19, 2018).

8. Quoted in Lee Colan, "A Lesson from Roy A. Disney on Making Values-Based Decisions," *Inc.*, July 24, 2019, https://www.inc.com /lee-colan/a-lesson-from-roy-a-disney-on-making-values-based -decisions.html.

9. Quoted in Ron Chopoorian and Daniel Gross, "Pfizer's Vaccine Machine, *Strategy+Business*, February 4, 2021, https://www.strategy -business.com/article/Pfizers-vaccine-machine.

10. Pfizer, "Our Values and Culture," *Pfizer 2019 Annual Review*, accessed October 8, 2021, https://www.pfizer.com/sites/default/files/investors /financial_reports/annual_reports/2019/our-purpose/our-values-and -culture/index.html.

11. Patrick M. Lencioni, "Make Your Values Mean Something," *Harvard Business Review*, July 2002, https://hbr.org/2002/07/make-your -values-mean-something.

12. Kathy Gurchiek, "Pfizer and SHRM CEOs Discuss COVID-19, Value of Culture," SHRM website, March 17, 2021, https://www.shrm.org /hr-today/news/hr-news/pages/pfizer-and-shrm-ceos-discuss-covid-19 -value-of-culture.aspx.

13. Emy Demkes, "The More Patagonia Rejects Consumerism, the More the Brand Sells," *The Correspondent*, April 28, 2020, https:// thecorrespondent.com/424/the-more-patagonia-rejects-consumerism -the-more-the-brand-sells.

14. Ron Carucci, "How Patagonia's Purpose Is Once Again Raising the Bar on Doing the Right Thing," *Forbes*, April 21, 2021, https://www .forbes.com/sites/roncarucci/2021/04/21/how-patagonias-purpose-is -once-again-raising-the-bar-on-doing-the-right-thing/?sh=66645d64777c.

15. A mission statement quoted in "Our Business and Climate Change" on the Patagonia Australia website, accessed October 8, 2021, https:// www.patagonia.com.au/pages/our-business-and-climate-change#:~ :text=Patagonia's%20mission%20statement%20reads%3A%20% E2%80%9CBuild,if%20we%20hope%20to%20survive.

16. Esha Chhabra, "Patagonia Rallies for an Earth Tax," *Forbes*, September 9, 2015, https://www.forbes.com/sites/eshachhabra/2015/09/09 /patagonia-rallies-for-an-earth-tax/?sh=9b5680a7340a.

17. Jeff Beer, "Exclusive: "Patagonia Is in Business to Save Our Home Planet," *Fast Company*, December 13, 2018, https://www.fastcompany .com/90280950/exclusive-patagonia-is-in-business-to-save-our-home -planet.

CHAPTER 4

1. Jen Karetnick, "Can The Prisoner's Dave Phinney Recapture Lightning in a Bottle?," *VinePair*, October 5, 2018, https://vinepair.com /articles/prisoner-wine-red-blend-phinney/.

2. Steve Curtin, "Hotel Guest Service: Being Capable Is Not Enough," *Hotel Business Review*, March 31, 2019, https://www.hotelexecutive .com/feature_focus/6018/hotel-guest-service-being-capable-is-not -enough.

3. Aaron Hurst, "30,000 Conversations Later: Hybrid Work Research Briefing," Imperative webinar, September 14, 2021.

4. Ryan Fuller and Nina Shikaloff, "What Great Managers Do Daily," *Harvard Business Review*, December 14, 2016, https://hbr.org/2016/12 /what-great-managers-do-daily.

5. Mark Horstman, "One-on-Ones," part 1 (Hall of Fame Guidance), *Manager Tools* podcast, July 3, 2005, https://manager-tools .com/2005/07/the-single-most-effective-management-tool-part-1.

CHAPTER 5

1. Noam Scheiber, "The Secret Lives of Hotel Doormen," *New York Times*, November 2, 2016, https://www.nytimes.com/2016/11/02 /business/service-with-a-human-touch-no-smartphone-can-do-that .html.

2. Scheiber, "Secret Lives of Hotel Doormen."

3. John Eades, "3 Lessons Every Business Can Learn from Chick-fil-A," *Inc.com*, April 18, 2017, https://www.inc.com/john-eades/why-chick -fil-a-is-crushing-the-competition-and-what-you-can-learn-from-it.html.

4. Kate Taylor, "Chick-fil-A Is Beating Every Competitor by Training Workers to Say 'Please' and 'Thank You,'" *Yahoo Finance*, October 3, 2016, https://finance.yahoo.com/news/chick-fil-beating-every -competitor-183200927.html.

5. Tricia McKinnon, "20 Things You Need to Know about Chick-fil-A's Success," *Indigo9 Digital* (blog), August 12, 2020, https://www .indigo9digital.com/blog/chickfilakeystosuccess.

6. McKinnon, "20 Things."

7. American Customer Satisfaction Index, *Restaurant Study 2020–2021* (Ann Arbor, MI: June 29, 2021), https://www.theacsi.org/images /stories/images/reports/21jun_acsi-restaurants-STUDY.pdf.

8. Nikki Waller, "What Tech Employees Want," *Wall Street Journal*, March 7, 2017, https://www.wsj.com/articles/what-tech-employees -want-1488856262.

9. VIPdesk, Customer Delight Guide: Top 10 Ways to Delight Your Customers Today! (n.d.), available at https://insights.vipdesk.com /customer-delight.

10. Robert E. Farrell, *Give 'em the Pickle!* (Portland, OR: Farrell's Pickle Production Inc., 1995).

11. Tom Rath and Donald O. Clifton, *How Full Is Your Bucket?* (New York: Gallup Press, 2004).

CHAPTER 6

1. Bruce Simpson, "Leading with Purpose and Humanity: A Conversation with Hubert Joly," *McKinsey Quarterly*, June 18, 2020, https:// www.mckinsey.com/business-functions/strategy-and-corporate -finance/our-insights/leading-with-purpose-and-humanity-a -conversation-with-hubert-joly.

2. Simpson, "Hubert Joly."

3. Patrick M. Lencioni, "Make Your Values Mean Something," *Harvard Business Review*, July 2002, https://hbr.org/2002/07/make-your-values -mean-something.

4. Toma Kulbytė, "37 Customer Experience Statistics You Need to Know for 2022," *SuperOffice* (blog), June 24, 2021, https://www.superoffice .com/blog/customer-experience-statistics/.

CHAPTER 7

1. David Shariatmadari, "A Real-Life *Lord of the Flies*: The Troubling Legacy of the Robbers Cave Experiment," *The Guardian*, April 16, 2018, https://www.theguardian.com/science/2018/apr/16/a-real-life -lord-of-the-flies-the-troubling-legacy-of-the-robbers-cave-experiment.

2. James C. Collins and Jerry I. Porras, "Building Your Company's Vision," *Harvard Business Review*, September–October 1996, https:// hbr.org/1996/09/building-your-companys-vision.

3. Donald B. Egolf and Sondra L. Chester, "Forming, Storming, Norming, Performing: Successful Communication in Groups and Teams," *iUniverse*, 3rd ed., June 24, 2013.

4. Tom Shales, "New Testament to Genius: Turner's 'Cecil B. DeMille,'" *Washington Post*, April 5, 2004.

5. Sarah Whitten, "Hollywood Doesn't Adjust the Box Office for Inflation, but If It Did, These Would Be the Top 10 Highest-Grossing Films of All Time in the US," CNBC, July 22, 2019.

6. Sunny Bonnell, "Why Your Company Needs a War Cry," *Inc.*, December 3, 2014, https://www.inc.com/young-entrepreneur-council/why-your-company-needs-a-war-cry.html.

7. Elizabeth Bernstein, "Say It Again, a Mantra Really Works," *Wall Street Journal*, May 9, 2017.

8. Sasha Frere-Jones, "As Is: Bill Withers Makes No Apologies," *New Yorker*, February 28, 2010, https://www.newyorker.com/magazine/2010/03/08/as-is-2.

9. Jim Manney, "Go Set the World on Fire," *Ignatian Spirituality* (blog), September 4, 2013, https://www.ignatianspirituality.com/go-set-the-world-on-fire/.

10. David Gelles, "Patagonia v. Trump," *New York Times*, May 5, 2018, https://www.nytimes.com/2018/05/05/business/patagonia-trump-bears-ears.html.

11. Nate Dvorak and Bryant Ott, "A Company's Purpose Has to Be a Lot More than Words," *Gallup Workplace* (blog), July 28, 2015, https://www.gallup.com/workplace/236573/company-purpose-lot-words.aspx.

12. "Thank You for Choosing to #OptOutside with Us," REI website, November 30, 2015, https://www.rei.com/blog/hike/thanks-for-choosing-to-optoutside-with-us.

13. Kenneth McFarland, *The Eagle Has Landed* (audio cassette), (Chicago: Nightingale-Conant Corp.), 1983.

14. "Symphony 101 FAQs," Symphony Nova Scotia website, https://symphonynovascotia.ca/faqs/symphony-101/why-do-the-musicians-play-a-few-notes-before-the-conductor-comes-on/.

15. Daniel Uthman, "The Special Offseason Workshops That Made Alabama Special," *USA Today Sports*, January 6, 2016.

CONCLUSION

1. James Clear, *Atomic Habits: An Easy and Proven Way to Build Good Habits and Break Bad Ones* (New York: Avery), 2018.

2. James Clear, "This Coach Improved Every Tiny Thing by 1 Percent and Here's What Happened," an excerpt from *Atomic Habits*, on James Clear's website, https://jamesclear.com/marginal-gains.

3. Eben Harrell, "How 1% Performance Improvements Led to Olympic Gold," *Harvard Business Review*, October 30, 2015, https://hbr.org/2015/10/how-1-performance-improvements-led-to-olympic-gold.

4. Harrell, "1% Performance Improvements."
5. Clear, "This Coach."
6. "Mark McGwire's 1998 Home Run Record Chase," MLB website, http://content.mlb.com/documents/5/3/4/269822534/mcgwire_1998 _stats.pdf.

Acknowledgments

2 020 was a tough year. I had my final event in Cambridge, Massachusetts, in early March and everything afterward either canceled immediately or was postponed and eventually canceled as the gravity of the pandemic was realized.

During this unsettling period, with my normal work routine interrupted, I thought it might be a good time to write a book. My wife, Julie, thought it would be a good time to get paid for something, but relented. I would like to thank her for her steadfast support of my decision, even though she knew this meant that she would lose her dining room table to stacks of papers and manila folders for the next nine months.

I would like to thank my literary agent, Michael Snell, who patiently listened to my ideas for this book over the course of several years as the outline took form. Michael helped me to create a proposal that attracted just the right publisher for this project.

Berrett-Koehler is a purpose-driven publisher whose mission is to connect people and ideas to create a world that works for all. More than a publishing company, it is grounded in thinking about how leadership plays a role in addressing today's pressing issues. Its priority is to support authors in getting their ideas onto paper or into a digital or audio file and into the hands of readers and listeners— and, ultimately, into practice in the communities they serve. I am grateful to have discovered them.

I wish to thank my developmental editor, Danielle Goodman. She took a metaphorical "shoebox full of ideas scrawled onto scraps of paper" and made sense of them. By sharing incisive (and sometimes, bruising) feedback and suggestions based on an early review of the manuscript, she made this a better book.

And because a picture really is worth a thousand words, I would like to thank my graphic designer, Scott Preator, for creating the book's eleven images that saved me from having to write (and you from having to read) another eleven thousand words.

And, finally, thank you to my editor, Neal Maillet, for his patience after I missed multiple deadlines. And for his creativity in keeping the book release very close to its original date, despite my tardiness.

Index

Note: *italicized* page numbers in this index indicate illustrative material.

G

GAAP (generally accepted accounting principles), 119
Gallup (management consulting company), 19, 20, 104
Garmin (technology company), 132
General Mills, 56
General Motors, 55
goals, aspirational, 65–66, 69
Goodman, John, 101
Google (search engine), 55
Google Docs (collaboration software), 83
Grail (healthcare company), 132

H

"happy accidents," 6
Harley-Davidson, 55
hobbies, 17
Horstman, Mark, 84–85
Hurst, Aaron, 83
Hyatt (hotel company), 52, 53, 58, 59, 61

I

IAG Limited (insurance company), 59
Ignatius of Loyola, 132
IKEA, 55
Imperative (peer coaching platform), 83
ING (financial services firm), 59
Inside the Magic Kingdom (Connellan), 24–25
inspiration, and team alignment, 135–136
integrity, 64
It's My Pleasure (Turner), 96

J

job essence
definition, 90
and job functions, 4, 29–30, 74, 91–97
and job purpose, 28–29
management of, 101–105
operationalization of, 97–99
job functions
contrasted with job essence, 4, 91–94
contrasted with job roles, 27–28, 31–32
definition, 90
and job essence, 29–30, 94–97
visible and concrete, 33–34
job knowledge, 6, 27–28, 37–39, 73, 74, 77, 91, 127
job priorities, 31–33, 35–37
job purpose
connections to actions and behaviors, 99–101
contrasted with life purpose, 5, 15–18
definition, 28
and employee engagement, 19–21
four questions to identify, 46–54
and job essence, 28–29
and job functions' contributions, 7
and organizational purpose, 45–46, 58–59
quantification of, 50, 52
job roles
overview, 27–31
and purpose, 26–27
jobs, definitions, 17
job skills, 6, 27–28, 37–39, 73, 74, 77, 91, 127
Joiner, Brian, 72–73
Joly, Hubert, 119

About the Author

STEVE CURTIN. After a twenty-year career at Marriott International working in operations, human resources, sales and marketing, and headquarters training and development, in 2007 Steve launched his own consulting company with the mission to influence the quality of customer service that is delivered by service providers and enjoyed by customers through speaking, writing, and consulting on the topic.

Steve's ideas about the links between customer service, employee engagement, and organizational purpose have made an impact on clients ranging from large corporations like T.J. Maxx, Carnival Cruise Line, and Marriott International, to nonprofits, government agencies, and tourism boards.

In 2013, Steve published his first book, *Delight Your Customers: 7 Simple Ways to Raise Your Customer Service from Ordinary to Extraordinary*. The book was inspired by his observation that while employees *consistently* execute the mandatory job functions for which they are paid, they *inconsistently* demonstrate voluntary customer service behaviors for which there is little or no additional cost to their employers.

Steve's latest book, *The Revelation Conversation: Inspire Greater Employee Engagement by Connecting to Purpose*, was inspired by the observation that while organizations *consistently* develop corporate mission, vision, and purpose statements, leadership is *inconsistently* able to recall them. As a result, leaders are unable to reveal these corporate ideals to employees, connect them to employees' daily job responsibilities, or leverage them to inspire greater employee engagement—until now.

Steve lives in Denver, Colorado, with his wife, Julie, their four children, and a Goldendoodle named Nugget.

Berrett–Koehler Publishers

Berrett-Koehler is an independent publisher dedicated to an ambitious mission: *Connecting people and ideas to create a world that works for all.*

Our publications span many formats, including print, digital, audio, and video. We also offer online resources, training, and gatherings. And we will continue expanding our products and services to advance our mission.

We believe that the solutions to the world's problems will come from all of us, working at all levels: in our society, in our organizations, and in our own lives. Our publications and resources offer pathways to creating a more just, equitable, and sustainable society. They help people make their organizations more humane, democratic, diverse, and effective (and we don't think there's any contradiction there). And they guide people in creating positive change in their own lives and aligning their personal practices with their aspirations for a better world.

And we strive to practice what we preach through what we call "The BK Way." At the core of this approach is *stewardship,* a deep sense of responsibility to administer the company for the benefit of all of our stakeholder groups, including authors, customers, employees, investors, service providers, sales partners, and the communities and environment around us. Everything we do is built around stewardship and our other core values of *quality, partnership, inclusion,* and *sustainability.*

This is why Berrett-Koehler is the first book publishing company to be both a B Corporation (a rigorous certification) and a benefit corporation (a for-profit legal status), which together require us to adhere to the highest standards for corporate, social, and environmental performance. And it is why we have instituted many pioneering practices (which you can learn about at www.bkconnection.com), including the Berrett-Koehler Constitution, the Bill of Rights and Responsibilities for BK Authors, and our unique Author Days.

We are grateful to our readers, authors, and other friends who are supporting our mission. We ask you to share with us examples of how BK publications and resources are making a difference in your lives, organizations, and communities at www.bkconnection.com/impact.

Dear reader,

Thank you for picking up this book and welcome to the worldwide BK community! You're joining a special group of people who have come together to create positive change in their lives, organizations, and communities.

What's BK all about?

Our mission is to connect people and ideas to create a world that works for all.

Why? Our communities, organizations, and lives get bogged down by old paradigms of self-interest, exclusion, hierarchy, and privilege. But we believe that can change. That's why we seek the leading experts on these challenges—and share their actionable ideas with you.

A welcome gift

To help you get started, we'd like to offer you a **free copy** of one of our bestselling ebooks:

www.bkconnection.com/welcome

When you claim your **free ebook**, you'll also be subscribed to our blog.

Our freshest insights

Access the best new tools and ideas for leaders at all levels on our blog at ideas.bkconnection.com.

Sincerely,

Your friends at Berrett-Koehler

Certified

Corporation